THE
HEALING
POWER OF
Singing

THE
HEALING
POWER OF

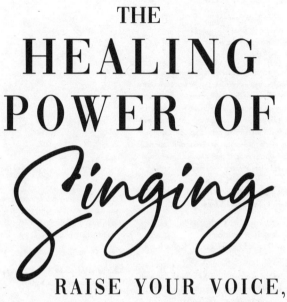

RAISE YOUR VOICE,
CHANGE YOUR LIFE

What Touring with David Bowie,
Single Parenting and Ditching the Music Business
Taught Me in *25 Easy Steps*

EMM GRYNER

ECW

Published by ECW Press
665 Gerrard Street East
Toronto, Ontario, Canada M4M 1Y2
416-694-3348 / info@ecwpress.com

Editor for the Press: Emily Schultz
Cover design: Angie Gauthier
Diagrams: Deni and Angie Gauthier, Second Records

The information provided in this book is designed to
provide helpful information on the subjects discussed.
This book is not meant to be used, nor should it be
used, to diagnose or treat any medical condition.
For diagnosis or treatment of any medical problem,
consult your own physician. The publisher and author
are not responsible for any specific health or allergy
needs that may require medical supervision and are
not liable for any damages or negative consequences
from any treatment, action, application or preparation,
to any person reading or following the information in
this book. References are provided for informational
purposes only and do not constitute endorsement of
any websites or other sources. Readers should be aware
that the websites listed in this book may change.

LIBRARY AND ARCHIVES CANADA CATALOGUING IN
PUBLICATION

Title: The healing power of singing : raise your
voice, change your life : what touring with David
Bowie, single parenting and ditching the music
business taught me in 25 easy steps / Emm Gryner.

Names: Gryner, Emm, author.

Identifiers: Canadiana (print) 20210214368 |
Canadiana (ebook) 20210215240

ISBN 978-1-77041-552-2 (softcover)
ISBN 978-1-77305-782-8 (ePub)
ISBN 978-1-77305-783-5 (PDF)
ISBN 978-1-77305-784-2 (Kindle)

Subjects: LCSH: Singing—Instruction and study. |
LCSH: Singing—Psychological aspects. | LCSH:
Voice—Care and hygiene. | LCSH: Voice—
Psychological aspects. | LCSH: Self-actualization
(Psychology) | LCSH: Gryner, Emm.

Classification: LCC MT820 .G894 2021 | DDC
783/.043—dc23

This book is funded in part by the Government of Canada. *Ce livre est financé en partie par le gouvernement
du Canada.* We also acknowledge the support of the Government of Ontario through the Ontario Book
Publishing Tax Credit, and through Ontario Creates.

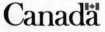

PRINTED AND BOUND IN CANADA   PRINTING: FRIESENS   5 4 3 2 1

To Liese

CONTENTS

Part 1

GETTING
STARTED

CHAPTER 1

THE BEGINNING

June 25, 2000
Worthy Farm, Pilton, Somerset, Glastonbury, UK

Steam rose from the mosh pit. Ecstatic faces, about a hundred thousand of them, fixed their gazes upon us as we walked onstage. A roaring wave of cheers rose to meet us, and I took my place in front of my mic. There were people as far as my eyes could see — and all together they looked like tiny flowers on a mammoth sheet of wallpaper. As I imagined filling this huge field with my voice, *he* emerged, slowly and full of great intention, to a second wave of cheers which engulfed the night sky. Dressed in a shimmering long blazer, his hair blond and tousled, his expression was both serious and bursting quietly with anticipation. The cheer that swept over all of us was deafening, a sound like nothing I'd ever heard. Human voices, maxed out and melted together, infused with love, euphoria, and, since they'd all been waiting for him for hours, great relief. The crowd noise blasted past my in-ear monitors. He stood front and centre and the rest of us, his backing band, inhaled. We shot looks of cockiness out to the audience — the way bands do when they are about to put on some kind of unforgettable spectacle of musical heroism. But there were smiles, too, and underneath it all, giddy disbelief. *How did we end up here?* I knew deep down that being on that stage, so high in the sky, in an idyllic corner of Britain at the turn of the millennium, was the stuff of rock 'n' roll majesty. We were on top of the world. And we were onstage with the man who had changed that world: David Bowie.

———

This book is about how I got to places like Glastonbury, but it also has clear tips on how to sing and what changes you need to make to your life to support your best voice. Through stories, diagrams, and action items that really worked for me, I tell you about my path as a singer in hopes that it sparks a few or many bright lights of inspiration for you.

People ask me all the time, "Can anyone sing?" My answer is yes. But then I follow it up with more good news: **You don't need to learn to become a singer as much as you need to uncover your inner singer.**

Most of the tools you need to make everything happen aren't hard to find. They are already in you. But the world insists on making things confusing. When it comes to learning the basics of singing, a mountain of advice is out there in videos, books, exercises, and so on. How on earth are you supposed to know what's right and what's wrong for you? How do you know what method is best? You may wonder, How long will it take? Is it even worth doing? Can I make a career out of singing? Where's my confidence? Why does my dog act unusual when I sing? Beneath the constant self-doubt we feel as a new singer, there's the stuff we tell ourselves — that this is *singing*, not aviation engineering or biomedical research — and thereby, right out of the gate, downgrade our dream. We become experts at coming up with every excuse on the planet as to why singing is not as important as our so-called grown-up responsibilities. Yet deep inside we know there is a voice aching to get out. That feeling has led you to pick up this book.

Let me tell you: you can do this.

BORN TERRIBLE

I was born a terrible singer.

I grew up in the Ontario countryside where I mastered the art of cleaning chicken poop off eggs and shimmying around house corners with a Nerf gun raised high, pretending to be Heather Locklear in the cop show *T.J. Hooker*. A lot of time was spent at the beach nearby, where I made poorly designed forts out of garbage bags and twigs — forts that made the Three Little Pigs' straw hut look like a doomsday bunker. My parents ran a newspaper out of our basement called *Feather Fancier*, a monthly publication devoted to the improvement of chickens. Whoever knew that chickens needed improving? My parents' business fed my two brothers and me and paid the family bills for 20 years. Poultry shows and long chats between my parents and other chicken enthusiasts were normal occurrences in my childhood. Never once did I question such commonly heard phrases as "sexing waterfowl" or "best cock in show."

I never sang when I was a kid. I knew nothing of pageant stages or reality-show singing contests, nor did I collect any trophies for singing at the local music festival. I was painfully shy, almost mute. At church, purely out of obligation, I grunted through hymns, ramping up the volume only a couple of decibels towards the end of the service, knowing that a bonanza of sugary treats awaited me at the variety store. Ask, and a box of Gobstoppers shall be given you; seek that pouch of Fun Dip, and ye shall find: Gryner 7:7.

Even though I didn't sing, our household was musical. My brothers and I were put into music lessons by our parents. I studied piano with an elderly lady named Miss Fawcett, and my lessons with her were excruciating. Every Monday after school, I'd trudge over to her tiny white house and push myself through a squeaky screen door, school bags in tow. Miss Fawcett would have homemade soup on the stove and the CBC playing on her fridge-top radio, and she'd leave both on a little too long as if to say, "Before *you* got here I was having the complete, most bitchin' time of my life."

Miss Fawcett's piano was pristine. When I sat down to play it, I wouldn't be 30 seconds into a sonata by some dead Italian and she'd be poking me really hard in the shoulder, telling me to "shove over" so she could show me how it was really done. "I've lived a full life!" Miss Fawcett would declare, masterfully arpeggiating up and down the keys as I sobbed quietly. "If you never practise, you'll never get anywhere!" I'm not sure to whom she was yelling this stuff, me or herself. Piano lessons became less of a run-through of my work and more of an exercise in positioning myself on the bench to cleverly hide my tears. Nine times out of ten, I'd leave her house feeling worthless. I'd climb into our family's talking Chrysler New Yorker, which told you in a 1984 robot voice if you'd left your "door ajar," and my dad, drinking beer wrapped in a brown bag, would zip me home to chicken world. These lessons lasted for eight long years.

———

In grade two, I overheard some girls in my class listening to "Physical" by Olivia Newton-John, and my ears couldn't help but perk up. Having been raised in the sticks, consumed by chickens, church, and TV, I had completely missed this kind of music. "You don't know this?" one girl said with a sneer to me as she pulled up her leg warmers. Feeling small, I decided to go home and find some of this peppy music that snobby girls loved, and find it I did.

A love affair exploded between me and everything on the radio. Pop, soul, and rock music wafted into my delicate ears from nearby Detroit radio stations. Then, in what I would classify as one of the high points of my kid life, I was allowed to stay up and watch the 1983 Grammy Awards. For the duration of the broadcast, I sat on the edge of our dark green velour couch, wide-eyed and full of glee. What was that crazy look in the eyes of Colin Hay, lead singer of Men at Work, who was jumping around singing about vegemite sandwiches and whatever else? Was it the magic of fame? The rush of live TV? A trillion cups of coffee? I didn't know. All I could hear were magical flutes, big cracking drums, and melody, sweet melody. Tina Turner, Stevie Wonder, Madonna, goddammit — even Mr. Mister — they all belonged to me. They were singing to me. A sheltered little country girl had found her salvation.

Inspired, I started to write my own songs. My first song was called "Dancing in the Leaves," an instrumental polka stiffer than dirty old roadkill. Despite its stilted simplicity and clear plagiarism of "Frosty the Snowman," my parents insisted this work was genius.

Around the time I turned 12, the desire to write about nature was quickly quashed by puberty. Ahh, yes — puberty. Maxi pads? With wings? Boys? Penises? Everything was new. Everything seemed uphill. Why were boys staring at me and saying stupid things? I felt like there had been a body swap in the night — a normal girl with dreams and talents had been switched with someone who had expanding body parts and a shrinking brain.

With music as my comrade, I forged on. I started writing love songs. There was one for Brad, a camp counsellor who was the spitting image of Duran Duran's John Taylor. Brad seemed to focus most of his attention on a blond girl at summer camp instead of me, so he got a song. There was one for Dani, a quiet boy with ice-blue eyes who showed up at our school one day, having moved from Alberta. Instead of paying attention to me, he would look out the school bus window, and as we all know, hell hath no fury like a woman who has been deemed less interesting than the same old shit that is going by the school bus window day after day. These tragedies were awarded some very energetic, heavy-pounding original piano songs that rivalled the unbridled rage of Survivor's "Eye of The Tiger" and Toto's "Hold the Line."

Things progressed. Around the time I turned 16, I started writing about other topics — my dad's coming-of-age in the Great Depression and his estrangement from his own father, for example. When two of my high school music teachers left their marriages to run off into the sunset together, that got a pretty sweet power ballad. I wrote about my own experiences of loneliness and isolation. Once upon a time, I'd have had to air my grievances in a flimsy Strawberry Shortcake diary or in a sad monologue to our house cat, Dusty, but suddenly, life was different. I was a woman. I was a songwriter. I could express everything through music and lyrics and nothing could hurt me. Every time I'd finish a song, I'd feel the weight of the world lifted from my tiny half-Filipino, half-Canadian shoulders. That weight turning into air and sorrow dissipating into blithe surrender are things I love about songwriting to this day.

Songwriting, however, wasn't enough for me. I wanted to record my songs. When my brother was away at jazz band practice, I'd sneak into his bedroom and pour all my ideas into his Fostex 4-track, a small recording device that predated the computer. I tried singing for the first time — really singing — and I loved what I heard when I played it back. I sounded different when I sang. I sounded new. I could put reverb on my voice — echo that went on forever, making me feel like I was singing in a big beautiful hall. When I was done recording, I'd set the faders — all four of them — back to zero and tiptoe out of my brother's blue-carpeted, blue-walled room, so proud of the hot tracks I had so covertly captured.

Writing songs and recording: there was nothing like it. From the middle of nowhere, I had found a boundless way to create worlds, air my frustrations, and see ideas spring to life. Still, I wanted more. I hadn't put all of my toil and tears into these songs to have someone else sing them. "I must sing my own songs," I'd say to myself into my bedroom mirror, spraying my bangs sky-high, "and I must be heard by the world." A look of stealth determination marked my purple Wet n Wild–eyeshadowed gaze.

Growing up in the 1980s meant no internet, and where we lived meant no friends nearby. One pastime we had we called "bottle hunting." My brothers would hike up and down the lakeshore road where we lived, collecting stubby beer bottles that people had thrown from their cars. My brothers used to collect bags and bags of cans and bottles and trade them in for sweet cash. While I never partook in this money-making scavenger hunt, I did walk up and down the same road. One day, I found a cassette tape labelled *Coney Hatch*. It had clearly been eaten by someone's car tape deck and swiftly thrown out the window. But I was curious, and I brought it home, put it back together with Scotch tape, and carefully wound it back into playable shape. I heard the sweet sounds of raw rock 'n' roll from a band that I had never heard on the radio. While my brothers laid claim to prog rock and guitar metal, I laid claim to this mysterious, peculiarly named Canadian band. I eventually searched out their other records at the store and figured out a way to contact one of the guitar players and writers, Carl Dixon.

Carl eventually wrote me back — it had been years since he'd received a fan letter — and told me all about his "long dry spell out of the game." He told me about his influences as a writer and guitarist — Small Faces, Little Feat, Ronnie Wood, Paul Rodgers. I felt a sort of kinship with this aging rocker, and I mailed him the recordings I had been making in my brother's bedroom.

Carl loved my songs and invited me into a studio to record them. This invitation blew my head off. I could have peed from joy. In fact, I probably did. A consummate gentleman and sincere mentor, Carl worked hard to make sure the five best songs I had written were recorded well. We talked about "taking a shot at the music industry" with these recordings, but his most influential advice came when he suggested that I take singing lessons.

Now. It's easy to take a suggestion like, "You should take some vocal lessons" to mean the person is really saying, "Let me wrap a duvet around my entire head so every time you open your mouth, it sounds like you're a couple thousand miles away." But I trusted Carl. He always struck me as a genuine music man. Not to mention, one of us had toured with Iron Maiden and it wasn't me, so I took his advice to heart. Sure, I loved singing, but I had to admit that my teenage voice was buried. When I sang, I'd tire easily and my voice would crack. Unlike the mountain of knowledge I had amassed about piano theory, I had no clue what I was doing when it came to singing. I didn't want to be terrible. If I was going to sing and reach the tippy-tops of the pop charts, I would have to take those lessons.

I said yes to vocal lessons, and saying yes changed my life.

———

By 21, I'd been living in Toronto already for a year. I had signed a worldwide record deal as a solo artist with Mercury Records. I felt incredibly excited and proud to sign those papers in my little second-floor apartment near Roncesvalles Avenue. The recording budget for my debut record would be $250,000 and my advance cheque, the first of two payments, was $75,000, all in U.S. dollars. There were plans for videos and radio singles. I was over the moon.

Then, in a totally separate opportunity, I got a job singing and playing keyboards in David Bowie's band. We jet-setted to Europe after playing on all the late-night shows that I used to watch as a kid — *Saturday Night Live, The Late Show with David Letterman* — and some I hadn't, such as *TFI Friday* and *Later with Jools Holland*. What's more, I got to fly to New York City a whole heck of a lot and rehearse with world-class musicians, all the while, singing an incredible catalogue of iconic music. I ended up recording with Bowie in the studio. I was in love with life. While this was going on, I was nominated for three Juno Awards for my own music — twice for Pop Album of the Year, alongside people like Leonard Cohen and Alanis Morissette. This was unprecedented for an independent artist at the time. I felt a little like I could laugh in the faces of the skeptics I had encountered along the way, and all those labels in Canada that didn't choose to sign me.

While it seems like success happened overnight, it really didn't. In the pursuit to get my deal, I'd had a few disheartening rounds of approaching labels. Sometimes acquaintances would pass around recordings I made to no reaction whatsoever. Other times, music execs would come out and see me play but then give the world's most useless feedback. "She needs to stand up when she's playing," one said when he came to a show where I sang and played my guitar while seated on a stool. "We've already got a female on our label," was another eye-roll-inducing thing I heard around that time. It wasn't until I won a songwriting contest, made an album with my prize money, and went and hired my own publicist that I got some attention in the States. The whole process of getting a deal, while it seemed quick, actually took about four years.

Among the highlights of my career over the years was playing concerts all over North America, Europe, and Asia. During one tour of the Philippines, I got to sing for my grandmother and my mother. It was a treasured moment in a beautiful, tropical land. I sang and acted in a feel-good feature film called *One Week* and also made a song with Canadian astronaut Chris Hadfield that would become the first music video ever shot in outer space. Making a version of "Space Oddity" for Hadfield's video was something I did while being a mom to two kids under the age of four.

Moral of the story: A kid from the middle of nowhere whose voice sounded like it was trapped inside an elephant's anus went on to become a great singer with pretty great experiences. What I did to get there, I share in this book.

YOUR TURN

You've started this book because you want to sing, you'd like to sing better, or you're curious about singing's healing magic. Why does anyone want to sing? Why does it make us feel so awesome? I could dive into the healing qualities of singing that science has laid out for us but in a nutshell, here's the lowdown: Singing has been shown to improve overall health and lower stress in the brain and body. Singing, especially with others, releases positive neurochemicals such as beta-endorphin, dopamine, and serotonin — the chemicals that increase feelings of happiness. Breathing deeply and consciously, the root of all good singing, has its own array of healing benefits. You can read up on the research, but none of this is necessary to know in any great detail as you move through your own practice. You will feel these benefits, even if the technicalities of the benefits are not catalogued in your brain. Aside from all the health benefits of breathing and singing, using your voice and expressing yourself can also fill a place in the heart and soul in a way that very few other things can or ever will.

Some people might argue that singing can't be taught in a book. Some might say that since we are all so unique, there is no one path to success that will work for everyone. Sure. Every human is unique, but in my long career as a performer and now a coach, I've seen singers commonly struggle with the same mental and physical hurdles time and time again. For these issues, there exist actual solutions that work. That's why throughout this book, I roll out 25 steps, or more accurately "secrets" I've learned through a life of singing. These secrets are woven within the stories and information I share. At the end of every chapter, I give a list of action items, which if followed can initiate transformation and spark inspiration depending on how far you want to explore each one. This book, along with working with the right vocal coach or exploring some of my vocal videos at emmgryner.com, will help you move into being your most confident singer. I provide tips and life lessons learned and proven through an actual career in music.

It's important for me to acknowledge that some of us have impediments, speech disorders, or medical conditions that make using our voice difficult. My claim that anyone can sing is not meant to be insensitive to those who have so far found they cannot or struggle with illness. But often those of us who have limits, self-imposed or circumstantial, can release ourselves in various ways from the hold those limitations put upon us. Singing is truly a miracle. There have been stories of people with no ability to speak who have found ways to sing. Studies have been conducted on people suffering from chronic obstructive pulmonary disease that show symptoms lessen and breathing capacity improves with weekly vocal lessons. People who experience stuttering can often sing without the stutter that affects their everyday speech. It's also important to note that the "gold standard" of singing is not set by the singing champions of music history — it is set by you. Letting go of preconceived ideas of what the "perfect voice" sounds like allows our own unique-sounding voice the freedom to expand. Letting go of perfection allows for joy.

The notion of "If a girl from the sticks can do it, anyone can" is only part of why I wanted to write this book. Much to my own surprise, the great discovery of my musical life was not actually what I learned in my vocal lessons or in the experience of singing with a rock legend . . . although those things were life-changing and I'll share plenty about the ins and outs of them as they relate to learning. But it was at age 42, as I was resting comfortably in what I perceived as a happy life — mothering, singing, being a wife, and recording albums — that life came crashing down. Crashing down in the worst possible way. Without warning or a chance to save it, my 16-year marriage ended. Grief engulfed me not only in the earth-shifting heartbreak of my family splitting apart (my children were four and six at the time) but also as a result of the deaths of a few dear friends, which happened around the same time. As if that wasn't enough, I found myself struggling financially, spiraling into a place of rage, destructive habits, and self-sabotage. Deeply hurt by how my life had shifted *way* out of my control, I made choices that drove me further into the ground. Just when I thought I knew everything there was to know about a music career and my own voice, about love and living, I found myself completely alone in the darkest time in my life.

It was as though the indie musician who had everything going for her had somehow ended up in a bad Lifetime movie. I felt disposable — discarded by my life partner, humiliated, and sad. Not only did I not have my family unit anymore, I was suddenly without the promise of 25th or 50th wedding anniversaries or the soft comfort of knowing my husband and I would grow old together, sharing in our children's triumphs and tribulations — just being there for one another. It was a blow I could not believe I had been dealt.

Most of us think or hope we will move through life exempt from major tragedies. I certainly thought that divorce and a broken family were things that would never touch me in a million years. When dark times hit me square in the gut, I mixed suffocating emotions with the shock that it was even happening in the first place. This feeling took over for years until enough was enough. I knew I had to find a way to do better, to be better. I thought of my children and my future and knew that if I didn't find some answers, I was going to die angry and miserable. I knew that my kids, whom I love so deeply, would suffer if I didn't pull out of the anguish and victimhood in which I found myself. I dreaded the thought of waking up every day, going through the motions, trying to make it look like I had things together. I began to wonder if I had, for many years, been in survival mode — trying to uphold that very illusion that I was self-sufficient. Self-help books, which I read in interminable succession, barely scratched the surface of my pain. I tried everything to find a path to healing — supplements, exercise, therapy, vacations, makeovers, nutrition plans — you name it. I begged the universe to show me how to do better.

Enter Emee Fink.

Emee Fink was a 17-year-old girl who liked to bake cakes. She also loved to sing. One day out of the blue, her mom approached me to ask if I would teach Emee singing. Now, let me make this clear — I wanted to teach as much as I wanted to be sprayed by a team of skunks right before a hot date. I viewed teaching as Certified Career Failure, something you do when record sales have dried up like eggs left too long in the frying pan. But I agreed, and Emee came to me for lessons. What unfolded surprised me to no end.

Gradually, I found myself delighted by how much I loved guiding Emee to discover her voice. Light began to spill through the smothering cloud cover. Through teaching Emee, it dawned on me. I already had what I always dreamed of: a voice so I could sing my songs. I had worked so damn hard to get it, and although I had it and had done great things with it, I had completely taken it for granted. When more people came to me for lessons, I started to get to know the voice I had. I started to be grateful for it. I became more and more fascinated by the human voice — its power and potential — and the more I treasured my voice, listened to it, and used it (and my story) as a guide for others, the more I witnessed myself actually heal.

Amazing changes were really happening, and they were blowing my mind. Beyond what teaching singing was bringing to my life, I noticed that my voice, how it sounded, how strong it was, what I could sing, how easy or difficult it was, was reflecting back to me aspects of myself that very few other things had the ability to reveal. I played back my new recordings and could hear that my voice was more open, stronger, and renewed. My concerts evolved into more meaningful events, and they began to sell out for the first time since my twenties. I remember the moment it dawned on me, in middle of the night in late 2018. "This is too simple," I said to myself. My voice had been there all along, yet, caught up in life and just trying to get by and make stuff happen, I had failed to see its healing power.

Today, my voice is stronger than ever. I coach singers and artists all over the world, from Prague to New York, Hamburg to Toronto. I've helped people realize their long-buried dreams, to sing songs they've secretly always wanted to sing, to find richness and power in their voices, and, perhaps most importantly, to find a new sense of confidence. Outside of coaching, I have been stretching my own musical muscle in new ways — on a jazz album, on new vocally stratospheric music with my rock band, Trapper. I started to give talks about transformation to women's groups and companies. This was a new way to use my voice that I had never imagined.

During mid-life awakening, I applied to be the afternoon drive host at a newly incarnated CBC radio station in London, Ontario. Once the size of a broom closet, the station had expanded to incorporate a full news team, a morning show, and an afternoon show. I didn't get the job, but I did get the call to regularly fill in for the current afternoon host. I was immediately ushered in and learned everything about interviewing people, cutting my own segments, and being on the airwaves, flying by the seat of my pants. I had flashbacks to the time when I was 17 when I entertained going to university for radio journalism. Now, I was stepping into my very own education and a new experience as an on-air host. It was thrilling. In my role on the radio, my voice carried the news of the day. I interviewed politicians, musicians, and everyday citizens, and I connected audiences with the stories of their communities. The response to my "radio voice" was overwhelmingly positive and brought a new sense of joy and accomplishment to my life. From all over the listening area, everyone from doctors to farmers chimed in on how perfectly suited for the radio waves my speaking voice was. Again — my voice. Taking me somewhere new.

BREAKING THROUGH

As I write this, I find myself living with a renewed, energized attitude, and I'm proud of my decisions. I'm healthy and surrounded by love. Music continues to be my joy, whether it's performing or coaching or anything in between. An ally had been living in my own body — this instrument with which I thought I had already done it all (how can you top singing with David Bowie, right?) — and it was reflecting back to me truth, power, and possibility. So here it is — a book for you. The most exciting part? What took me over two decades to learn will only take you a fraction of the time: **clarity, resilience, confidence, and hope can all be yours through uncovering your voice**.

If you're reading this, you are searching for more. You want to sing. But maybe you are looking for a path alongside that journey that will lead to more joy. You know somewhere inside you that you need to make a lifelong dream a reality. You are looking for answers as to why your voice doesn't sound the way you want it to, why it doesn't do the things you want it to do, why it won't go high, or hold notes for long periods of time, or be strong — you're hoping that someone (me) knows what the heck she is talking about. I do.

I know the pain of not knowing the first thing about singing. When I was a teenager and couldn't sing well, my faith was high but my heart was breaking. The earnest words I'd written lay flat on the page and I couldn't sing well enough to bring those lyrics to life. Not having a strong voice felt like a life compromised, a life not lived. Later in life, unaware of myself and my potential, I'd stumble through my concerts — unchallenged, ungrateful, and flailing. It took the debilitating effects of divorce and grief for me to see my life's problems, to own them and make change.

I hear you and I see you. You want so badly to find your unique voice, to have it be heard and adored, but you have no clue if or how any of it can happen. You aren't sure where to start. You aren't sure that you are even supposed to be singing. You wonder if you will be judged and if you will be loved, or even liked!

The good news is you are ready. You are supposed to be singing. You will get to a place where judgments will have little to no effect on you. You will be and feel loved because you will get closer to loving yourself. It sounds hokey, but it's true.

There are a lot of stories in this book. Because I believe in what I've learned through my own experiences — from the technical to the trivial, the humorous to the heart-breaking — I use my stories to guide you in your own work. This book applies to everyone: I met a therapist who wished his speaking voice was stronger so that he could better communicate meaningful guidance to his clients. I gave voice lessons to an attorney in Manhattan who opened himself up to learn what singing could teach him. I've coached teachers, accountants, medical professionals, recording artists, massage therapists, IT professionals, and I've witnessed incredible transformation in every one of them. This is where my joy becomes immeasurable, seeing the change in others.

YOU DESERVE THIS

You deserve to be heard.

You deserve to uncover the dreams you pushed aside for other things.

You deserve to let go of the criticism from the past.

You deserve the chance to be strong in your life.

You deserve to live a life of clarity and deep connection.

I believe all of this starts with the voice.

I've lived the singer's life. I've sung through tears, rain and windstorms, with drums pounding in my ears, at funerals and weddings, in stadiums, on river boats, in ice cream shops, atop old train bridges, in boardrooms to jaded executives, in school rooms to wide-eyed students, and in recording studios all over the world. I sang on late-night TV, radio shows, air shows, coffee shops, gruelling video shoots, and in dirty bars with penises doodled in Sharpie on the wall. I've rushed to sing my last note so I could race home to breastfeed my baby. I've watched people like Bowie transform moments before going onstage. I've warmed up my voice hundreds of thousands of times. I've learned the hard lessons about drinking alcohol and singing. I've sweated through the national anthem at an NBA all-star game, crooned my babies to sleep, and sung myself through long drives between concerts simply to stay awake and alive.

The bottom line? **When our voices are not clear, our lives are not strong** and vice versa. You can and will uncover your inner voice. Set aside what you know about singing and what you fear about opening your mouth and making sound, and simply consider the notion that change is possible. Your voice is a gateway to finding your true self, and it's this connection with self that leads us to be more connected with others. I believe that positively connecting with the self and with others is life's greatest gift.

Dive in. Believe that something greater awaits you. While you inhabit this beautiful, expansive earth, let your unique voice be heard. Don't let it die with you.

Now is your time.

CHAPTER 2

REDISCOVER
YOUR BREATH

*"Take a deep breath and tell us your deepest, darkest secret,
so we can wipe our brow and know that we're not alone."*
— ALAN WATTS

ADULTS RUIN EVERYTHING

When you came bolting out of your mother's vagina, you were perfect. Equipped with a beating heart, lungs that worked, and no particular feelings about who is poised to win the Super Bowl, you were living in the moment. You also knew how to fill a room with the shrillest, loudest cry on earth. As a baby, without even knowing it, you were making sound with the maximum power available to you, using all the most powerful tools in your body. Every scream was being pushed out from the abdominal region. Adults, desperate to show the world that they know how to tame the Tasmanian devils to which they gave life, or who just want to eat a breakfast sausage in relative silence, make it their mission to quiet their children. "Use your indoor voice," adults say to kids.

As we learned to cooperate and be in the world, we subdued strong voices and grew into adults with a more socially acceptable way of making sound. But the time has come to take back our perfection, and we do so by breathing the optimal way, the way we did when we first came bolting from the womb.

All of which leads me to my first secret of singing: **Secret No. 1: Rediscover your breathing.**

The first and most important thing I learned in my vocal lessons was to rediscover my breath. Throughout the early years of learning to sing, my attention was scattered but I was determined, dressing up in shiny little dresses and big platform boots, playing live, belting out my own songs, and meeting whomever I could in the Toronto music scene. But even as a major label artist and a member of Bowie's band, I was still very much learning. Excitement over life and music was my fuel. You could say I learned as I went.

No matter your age or where you are in your singing experience, this is a wonderful time for you to do the same — learn as you go. Try a bunch of things — a vocal lesson, a choir practice, a karaoke night — and start seizing opportunities that relate to singing.

But as you try these different things, remember to keep tuning in to your breathing. Skipping over Secret No. 1 will make the other 24 secrets a bitch to embrace.

The questions I have fielded as a teacher are often the same:

"How do I stop singing out of tune?"

"How do I get power and hold long notes?"

"Why does my voice sound so weak?"

"Where did my falsetto voice go?"

"How do I build confidence as a singer?"

All of the answers to these questions are rooted in breathing. **To be great singers, we don't need to learn a new way of breathing, we need to rediscover what we were doing right in the beginning.** Am I suggesting that at this point in your life you'll land on the right breathing technique by screaming for your lamb stuffy and rolling around in a dirty diaper? No, unless that's something that would make you happy. There's a better way. Not only did we use the right muscles as babies to be vocally strong, we also partially use them now at night when we are sound asleep. More on this shortly.

CONSCIOUS SINGING

While learning to sing, it will help if you see yourself as a *conscious singer*. Being a conscious singer means that for a while you'll need to use your brain to absorb some slightly academic concepts. Eventually, your brain will be returned to passive duty — I promise! — and the joy of belting out Wilson Phillips in the car at full volume will return. But while you are on this journey, make a decision to be a "conscious singer" — a student once again.

Many people, maybe even some of your favourite artists, sing unconsciously. Before the age of 19, I also sang unconsciously. I was singing for fun, and I didn't know what I was doing. I used my throat and upper lungs to generate and control most of the sound. Some people figure they sound good enough and carry on singing this way for many years. The trouble with singing unconsciously, in addition to all the vocal cord wear and tear that could occur, is that in doing so, we fail to make use of the full potential the body possesses for breath, vocal power, and range. Due to the size and strength of the diaphragmatic and abdominal muscles, it makes far more sense to focus on this region and experience singing as a full body activity. By supporting the sound properly, there is a higher chance for good tone and expression and better overall performance.

Let's take a moment to understand our instrument. Please note: I never so much as thought about the inner-workings of my voice until much later in life. I was way too busy gluing fake eyelashes on my eyelids, romancing bodyguards, and snoring on tour buses as they rolled treacherously across the Rocky Mountains to care about any of this. Sure, style and presentation are part of singing. I do, however, believe that I would have become a stronger singer more quickly had I focused on how my body worked. So, assuming that you would rather see results quicker than two and a half decades, I encourage you to pay attention to this chapter.

OUR INSTRUMENT

When Doug from down the road gets a shiny new Fender Telecaster, he receives all the oohs and aahs in the world. He posts nine thousand pictures of it from different angles, polishes it with a shammy, and gives it an embarrassing pet name like Ramblin' Ruby or the Blues Machine. When it comes to the voice, no one is posting pictures of their esophagus, wiping down their neck a hundred times a day with cashmere, or naming their vocal cords Lenny. Maybe it's time we did. Or, you could just recognize and appreciate the incredible instrument that is your voice.

Because our instrument is inside our bodies we tend to be a bit "out of sight, out of mind" about it. We singers can be artists and dreamers. We romanticize making music and singing our hearts out. We've been known to say that our voice has been placed in us by a higher power. We figure if this is the case, we can down a couple of slippery elm lozenges and wow our family with a bitchin' take on "Zat You, Santa Claus?" at the next holiday dinner. But before you drift away into a singing utopia filled with floating unicorns and a sense of "this is my destiny," you need to know **Secret No. 2: Singing is a sport.**

Anyone who has become good at any sport has spent an exorbitant amount of time training. Training involves understanding the mental and physical aspects of the job at hand. Learning about your own physiology, especially as a creative type, can be a real recipe for a nap for some people, but just as an athlete would be acquainted with her own anatomy and, subsequently, her ability to elevate her skill to championship levels, education is key.

Nearly all athletes have a coach. Even though I coach singers, I have a coach too. Having my own vocal instructor allows me to be a better teacher to the singers with whom I work. My coach is this man, Mitch Seekins:

I found Mitch when the long-haired Carl suggested I take vocal lessons. Some friends of mine who were dabbling in singing out in the world were going to Mitch, so his name was floating around as *the guy* to go to for singing lessons. I took a leap of faith and gave him a phone call. Mitch would end up changing my life just as the vocal coach you choose will change yours (in Chapter 4, I address how to pick the right vocal coach). Although I've studied with Mitch on and off since age 19, I could have easily learned from him in my thirties, forties, or later. This is because singing is for all people of all ages. Mitch, the man who changed my life, agrees that seeing singing as a sport increases your chances of success.

"Singing is a coordination of muscles," explains Mitch. "Train, stay in shape, take care of your body like an athlete. You have to respect the instrument more than any other instrument because it's a part of you."

PART OF YOU

So exactly how is our instrument a part of us?

First, let's examine how sound is made. In order to make sound, you need:

- a source of power,
- something that vibrates,
- a place for the sound to resonate within,
- a way to transmit sound, and
- a way to receive sound.

We've all heard of the larynx. If your lungs are a palace, the larynx is the night watchman of that majestic palace.

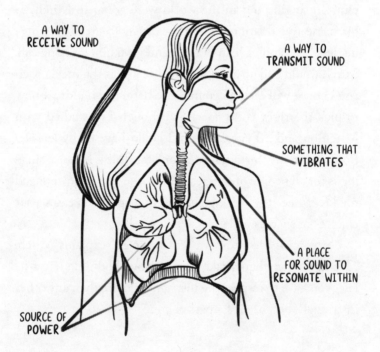

A WAY TO RECEIVE SOUND

A WAY TO TRANSMIT SOUND

SOMETHING THAT VIBRATES

A PLACE FOR SOUND TO RESONATE WITHIN

SOURCE OF POWER

The larynx's job is to be on the lookout for riff-raff and keep it out. By now, your larynx has probably already stopped a bunch of things from falling into your lungs — cherry pits, ice cubes, molars, small bugs, and so on. Let's hear it for the larynx! The larynx also contains the vocal folds and therefore is responsible for helping to create sound. We know this because when we have this inflammation of the larynx — laryngitis — we are hoarse or sometimes can't make sound at all. Unlike the act of breathing, where we can see and hear our lungs at work, we have no proof that the larynx is doing anything because we can't see it and we can't feel the muscles inside it. So, I suppose the larynx is more a night watchman in an invisibility cloak. Stay with me.

The trachea, or windpipe as some like to call it, is the majestic hallway that connects the invisibility-cloaked night watchman (larynx) to the palace (lungs). It is part of the vocal tract that allows for sound to resonate, and it allows air to flow between the lungs and the outside world.

Our vocal folds are awe-inspiring little puppies. When a soprano is belting out an aria, her vocal folds can vibrate at speeds of around two hundred times per second. This is why we can often hear a soprano sing over an orchestra with ease. (In normal speech, the folds vibrate at about half that speed). With these folds so active when we sing, a warm-up will be crucial to your practice.

Air itself is a magical, mystifying thing. Life cannot exist without air and oxygen. We have the ability to take in air and transform it into sound. Sound, turned into music, has the power to dismantle or inspire us, change the way we feel, and save us in the darkest of times. *You* have the ability to harness and radiate this power. So, maintaining a curiosity about how the body and the vocal cords work in relation to singing can give your practice more meaning, and the more meaning your practice has, the less likely you'll be to give it up for soap carving. **Secret No. 3: Stay curious.**

All of the magic, potential, and wonder of the human voice, this fascinating part of us that creates sound, exists in a relatively compact space in a human, but none of it means anything without its source of power. If the lungs are the palace, then the source of power, the abdominal region, is an army of strong women and men who keep the palace guarded, amped up, and running smoothly. And now, what you've been waiting for, a hand-drawn diagram to better communicate this "your lungs are a palace" metaphor:

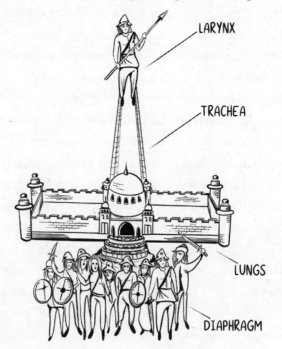

SO, LET'S TALK ABOUT THE
SOURCE OF POWER

Here's an analogy not brought to you by Mensa: If you were going on a cross-country road trip in your car, would you put a quarter tank of gas in or pump gas till it's full? You would fill it. The same is true with singing and breathing. When we sing only with our upper lungs and control the sound with the throat, we are only running on a quarter tank, if that. When we ignore the body's full capacity for breath, we end up giving out-of-tune performances that lack power and expression. Notes aren't held, the voice "cracks," the upper register suffers, and injuries happen.

So how do we tune in to a deeper kind of breathing and apply it to singing? The answer begins with the diaphragmatic muscle.

First, let's take a look at this beauty:

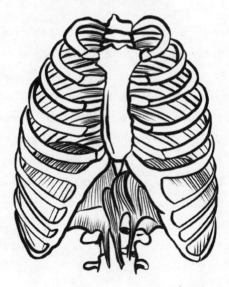

I was halfway through life and had sung "Crazy Train" as a ballad about two hundred times before I even knew what the diaphragm looks like. You don't really need to know what the diaphragm looks like to be a good singer, but if we want to stay curious and stay thankful for our instrument, it's worth knowing what wig-shaped fibres are swaying around inside you as you move through your day.

For the purpose of this book, I will call breathing with the diaphragm *belly breathing*. Some singers believe that belly breathing is a form of controlling the way they breathe but as I mentioned earlier, we have done this breathing from the day we were born so belly breathing is way less about control and more about becoming reacquainted with our bodies and relaxing into them again.

WHAT DOES BELLY BREATHING FEEL LIKE?

Belly breathing really is breathing with your diaphragm. It is commonly done in yoga. It can be done as part of relaxation exercises and sometimes during meditation. Belly breathing, or deep breathing, is often prescribed as a tool to reduce panic and anxiety. The benefits of this type of breathing, as seen through other kinds of intensive breathwork, extend to a lowered heart rate, lower blood pressure, lower stress levels, a realignment of the nervous system, and general good health. Tuning in to the diaphragmatic muscle and rediscovering how to breathe allows us to strengthen our power as singers while opening us up to a world of better health. Let me say that one more time: **tuning in to belly breathing allows us to strengthen our power as singers, while opening us up to a world of better health.**

It works like this: When we inhale, our belly comes out. When we exhale, it contracts.

At first, this kind of breathing can seem counter-intuitive. We are so accustomed to taking a breath in and watching our upper body and rib cage suck in to itself. But when we allow our shoulders, our upper body, jaw, arms, and most importantly our overactive minds to relax, we can flip the switch. Instead, we can inhale, see and feel the belly rise, and then exhale, seeing and feeling it come into the body.

Because seeing this in action is often more helpful than reading about it, I have posted a video of belly breathing on my site at emmgryner.com/videos.

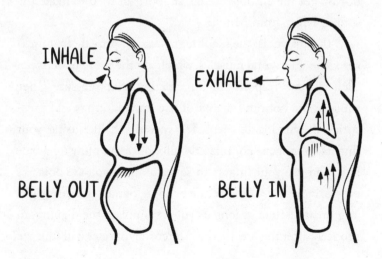

INHALE

EXHALE

BELLY OUT

BELLY IN

INTERCOSTALS

More news: The diaphragm does not work alone. We also have intercostal muscles that work in tandem with breathing to make optimal sound. Mitch explains:

"When you sing there are 2 phases. The breath phase, then the singing phase. You must breathe before you sing, and when you sing you are not breathing. Most people understand the proper way to breathe is to use diaphragmatic breathing. But then they are told that they then have to 'sing' with the diaphragm. The singer will take a diaphragmatic breath, then you have to sing with it? It's very confusing . . . and the result is, most singers will then use the abdominal muscles to sing with, because it gives the illusion of using the diaphragm while singing. Using the abs like that doesn't work well and is actually limiting and destructive vocally."

So how *do* you use the diaphragm while singing? How do you get the air pressure or "support" needed to make the sound? More from Mitch:

"The answer is: the diaphragm *does not* provide that pressure. The intercostal muscles, which are the muscles between each rib, are responsible for creating that pressure. They squeeze the bottom portion of the inflated lungs and pressurize the air inside them. It's very much like using your fingers to squeeze an inflated balloon. If you blow up a balloon and use your fingers to squeeze it, all you are doing is pressurizing the air inside the balloon. Same basic principle. You breathe, then as long as you manipulate the diaphragm properly after the breath, the intercostal muscles will squeeze the bottom of the lungs providing the needed air pressure to sing as effortlessly as possible."

Feeling overwhelmed? Just focus on the first step: understanding belly breathing.

Which brings me to my next point: Even though rediscovering your breath can be an empowering tool and an exciting concept to start working on, it's very likely the stage where you'll wanna close up the book, scoop yourself a bowl of chocolate gelato, and go shop online for soft jeggings and aromatherapy necklaces. But don't lose hope. When we lose hope, we lose interest, sometimes for good. There are two reasons trying to wrap your head around breathing brings about a block. The first is physical. Rediscovering your breathing and becoming a conscious singer means you are toning muscles you haven't bothered to think about, maybe ever. Toning and strengthening muscles does *not* happen overnight. It doesn't happen in a week, or a month, or even six months. And when people are slow to see results, they give up. The second reason is mental. Singing is supposed to be fun. Sometimes it's the only fun thing we do in our day. Suddenly, as I mentioned before, we find ourselves "back at school." We discover we have to use our brains to understand how to do all of this, which flies directly in the face of the great fun we used to have. Suddenly, belting out "Rock You Like a Hurricane" at full volume in the shower doesn't feel quite as enjoyable with all these dos and don'ts. This leads me to **Secret No. 4: You'll be able to forget this stuff one day.**

Everything you learn about proper singing technique will become second nature once you do it for a while. All of this thinking and coordination and brain power will fade away when you walk onstage and start really *feeling what you are singing*. When you drive a car, after many years of doing it, you're not thinking of the rules of the road. Instead, you enjoy the scenery of your trip, you listen to music or you passive-aggressively tell the passenger next to you to "feel free to nap" because secretly you don't want to make conversation with them. In fact, in those special moments, you sometimes don't even know you're driving a car! The same is true for singing. Trust. You'll be able to forget all of this stuff one sweet day.

ROCK SCHOOL

Right after high school, I went to rock school. There, alongside 60 long-haired dudes, I learned an introduction to music production. The program was actually called Music Industry Arts at Fanshawe College in London, Ontario, and I got the chance to record in studio with Jack Richardson, a brilliant, bubbly, round man who had produced records by legends Alice Cooper and Bob Seger, among others. As I continued my vocal lessons with Mitch, I recorded in the studio at school. I didn't know what I was doing, but I was having the time of my life — cutting drums at 3 a.m., downing bad caffeinated drinks, and writing big rock songs.

I also took my singing outside of the studio. I remember at one Battle of the Bands I was in, Jack was a judge. I stepped up onstage, wailed away, and trotted off backstage thinking I had crushed my performance like a big diva.

Jack came up to me later in a corridor and shook his head

at me. "Emm," he said, "you're singing way too high. The keys are too high for you. You need to lower them." And with that, he walked away. I was knocked down from a place of self-adoration, overwhelmed that in addition to singing, there were all these other factors about performing that I had yet to learn. I committed to work harder to understand my voice. I dropped the keys down. I tried to feel my way through the music. I tried to smooth out my rough voice. The problem was not solved. I was *still* not hearing my voice come to life. This sucks, I lamented. What do I have to do to be good?

Eventually, when I learned to use the whole source of power — combining belly breathing with the use of the intercostal muscles — things began to change. I was no longer just getting by at my concerts, or hoping I might make it through a difficult phrase of a song, I was making it through and doing it well. I gained confidence because I understood what was happening in my body. I trusted that my body would not let me down. I also exercised some patience.

More good news came. I found I could also make it through a show when I was sick, because singing properly takes the strain off afflicted areas. (I'll address singing through sickness later.) Using the source of power also changed my songwriting, because I started to write melodies that went higher, and lower, and incorporated notes that could be held longer. My shows became more dynamic and interesting. Because my audience loved the variety in melody, rhythm, and song I could now bring to the shows, they became a more responsive crowd. Once I rediscovered my breathing and learned how to support the sound, I could go onstage 100 percent sure I was going to give my best. Today, I leave my shows and my studio projects exhilarated. I hope my audience leaves the same way. It all began with belly breathing.

So how do you do this? You can begin to tune in to belly breathing right now. Once you get the hang of it, it will be with you for a lifetime. If you are already a singer and suspect you aren't singing consciously, don't despair. Scientific studies tell us that it takes an average of 66 days to see a new habit come to life. You can do this.

For some people, the best way to engage belly breathing is through intense concentration. For others, it's by completely zoning out. Some people will try to feel it working and won't for several attempts, and others can feel movement right away, even in small increments. So, give yourself a little room and grace to explore the following exercises.

EXERCISE 1

1. Rest your hand gently below the bottom of your rib cage, in the centre, just above your navel.
2. Take a normal breath, the kind of breath you take in the middle of your busy work day. Usually this breath is somewhat shallow — your shoulders and upper chest rise and suck in when you breathe in and fall and extend when you breathe out. Take that kind of breath now, without judgment. Inhale and then just let everything out and relax your body.
3. Now that you've taken that breath in Step 2 and have fully exhaled, inhale deeply *without* raising your shoulders or allowing your upper chest

to expand. This directs your air down. The diaphragm should flatten and, when that happens, your belly should expand.
4. Exhale and the belly should come *into* your body. The diaphragm returns to its natural shape.
5. Repeat Steps 3 to 4 as many times as you like to get the hang of it.

EXERCISE 2

1. Lie on your back on your couch or on the floor.
2. Place a book or a small object on your belly.
3. Breathe in and watch the book or object rise.
4. Breathe out and watch it lower. Diaphragmatic breathing. Lying down, but still diaphragmatic.

———

The above exercises might feel challenging at first. If you tried them both and felt nothing, resist the urge to whip this book into the recycling bin. About half of my students do not feel any movement when they try the exercises for the first time. But after some time, you will feel something. Perhaps after viewing the breathing video on my website, or watching it in action with your own vocal teacher, you can start to see a little progress. Remember that we are awakening a muscle, so it's not going to feel strong at first.

If you had some success with the exercise, you may feel winded or weak. Some people notice they feel lightheaded. With this exercise as well as all strategies and tips in this book, I encourage you to take baby steps. If you feel light-headed, stop, sit down, and take a break. Drink some water. In all cases, listen to your body. However, if there's any singing exercise to start working on to guarantee real improvement — this is the one.

Congratulate yourself if you actually put this book down and tried one or two of the above exercises: you are on your way towards unlocking a universe of possibility as a singer. If you skimmed the exercise or decided now is not the right time to try it, just jump back up and do the exercise. Do one round; it only takes 30 seconds to a minute. Make a little time for your awesome new creative work.

DAILY LIFE

Once you feel you've got this sort of breathing down, even in a small way, incorporate it into daily life. This regular use of your abdominal muscles and diaphragm will start to become second nature to you. You will also begin to strengthen and tone these muscles, just as anyone who goes to the gym tones their body through repeated activity and following a plan.

You can do belly breathing while you are doing other tasks. I can think of a host of places you can practise without dropping the falafel wrap you're holding. You can breathe this way while doing the dishes, walking the dog, or driving to work. You can belly breathe while binge-watching your favourite series, baking a rhubarb pie — heck, you can be working on your breathing as you're reading this book. Cultivate a sense of relaxation, follow your instincts, and return to what is natural for your body. **Breathing is not** an activity to force, but an activity to soften into, to relax into. So to recap, relax into your breathing and then start training like you're going into the Olympics.

ACTION ITEMS

1. **Start seeing singing as a sport.** Start thinking about getting a coach; treat your body like an athlete. Your instrument is *on* you, so that means you need to be more vigilant than someone who is learning guitar or piano. Your health will directly affect the health of your voice.

2. **Watch a video or get a little bit more familiar with diaphragmatic breathing.** It's easy to be reluctant or frightened by new concepts, but remember, you *already* do this. Seeing someone, anyone, do this breathing will open your mind to how you can do it too.

3. **Place your hand on your diaphragm and try three rounds of low breathing.** Let your shoulders drop and allow your belly to expand as you breathe in. Find what works for you, whether it's concentrating or zoning out. A tiny bit of movement is okay, and if you feel nothing, try again in a few minutes or even at a later time.

CHAPTER 3

SEE IT ALL HAPPENING

"The future you see is the future you get."
— ROBERT G. ALLAN

DRAWING THE GRAMMY

It was 1993. Enrolled in Music Industry Arts, I was record-ing every spare minute I had — sometimes in the studio and sometimes at my apartment. When other girls my age put on miniskirts and tank tops and headed to Richmond Row in London hoping to capture a fresh-faced university boy for the night, I was working away in a basement apartment recording songs on my own 4-track recorder, dreaming of something else. Was I the coolest 19-year-old on the planet? Probably not, but I was having my own kind of fun.

In Music Business Contracts class, surrounded by sleepy-eyed guitar players, new wavers, and music nerds, I would find myself listening intently to Professor Terry McManus. Terry, whose most notable claim to fame had been helping Mr. Dressup get out of a bad recording deal and then going on to tour with the popular kids' entertainer, was the funniest teacher I ever had. He had pants that came up to his chest, the most generous smile, and so much wisdom. His wisdom came from a very long career as a singer-songwriter, advocating for songwriters' rights in Canada, and, yes, from, as he remarked several times in class as though it had been a stint in the mafia, "working with Dressup."

Terry talked about the importance of being sure of where you were going. He asked us all one day, "Who in this class, except the person who drew a picture of themselves receiving a Grammy award, has pictured what they want to do in their life?" Terry snuck a glance at me. A smile crept over my face as my eyes darted left and right in a mix of pride and humiliation. I had drawn that picture and given it to Terry.

I knew where I wanted to go. Did I know if I would get there? Not really, but I knew I would get somewhere.

This early exercise of drawing myself receiving an award was simply: *visualization*. Visualizing success is a topic many people want to tune out, because it's often delivered by a Tony Robbins–type of motivational coach and followed up by a pitch to buy into some program that will change your life. But visualization actually works. I ask everyone with whom I work to complete a vision board, which leads me to **Secret No. 5: See it all happening.**

I don't know what it is about being an artist, a singer, or a musician that puts us in a floaty state of perpetual contemplation. We keep a part of ourselves locked away and there, under the shadows of life, reside our wildest dreams. Unfortunately, sometimes we really do end up keeping our dreams wild — untouchable and out of reach — as though they will draw us into some netherworld of ridiculous behaviour. We convince ourselves that the moment has passed, and the things we wanted, those dreams and aspirations, were just stuff on a checklist for our much younger, embryonic selves. Unless you actually died already, which would make it very difficult to explain how you are reading this, your dreams are achievable.

When we create a tangible version of our dreams as singers, we create a destination. Although the destination isn't the point of our singing life, visualizing the end point of our work provides us with a road map that can be useful throughout our training, growth, and self-discovery. The higher we shoot in our visions and the bigger we dream, the more likely we are to achieve the things we have secretly buried. While the Grammy hasn't made its way onto my shelf yet, I amassed a bagful of other awards and experiences, some that mean more to me than any trophy.

MY VISUALIZATION EXPERIMENT

In 2011, after many years of touring and recording as a solo artist, I took a little time out to dream up a musical trio of women. I was expecting my second child, and in an ultrasound, I had been informed that the baby's private parts, under the magnification of medical imaging, "looked like a mini cheeseburger," and therefore that meant my baby was female. (The boy version of this is a "turtle," apparently.) Anyway, at the mention of the word cheeseburger, I cried tears and tears of joy. Suddenly, I had a real reason to challenge my own beliefs about what it meant to be a woman.

Soon I would be guiding one, I'd be the mom of one! From that mention of the cheeseburger in my belly, I began celebrating women in a new way. I thought about our unique experiences, the way life and society force us into being resourceful and resilient and that we also have fun and share bonds like nobody else. I wanted that energy in a band. It was something I never had before. I channeled these feelings into a project where the voices and lyrics of women were front and centre.

At first I thought I'd create the band and produce it, but the more I thought about it, the more I thought, "I want to be in it!" I imagined a female version of Crosby, Stills, Nash & Young. I loved the intervals of those vocal harmonies, and I could envision a band of women masterfully playing things like banjo and fiddle and singing in ways that harkened back to the '60s and '70s. One of the earliest activities I did with this band, which was called Trent Severn, was paste together a future vision of us. This exercise cost me zero dollars, and it was one of the most important things that I did at any stage in my career for any project.

First, I found a photo online of a stage with thousands of people looking at it. I photoshopped our band banner onto the back of it. Next, I printed out images of three women — one with a fiddle, one with a banjo and one with a bass guitar — and cut and pasted them onto the stage, evenly spaced, as though we were performing to this massive crowd of eager onlookers. I took a photo of this collage, and it became the vision for the band. I shared the photo with my bandmates, put it in a scrapbook, and kept it on my computer.

In 2017, the vision came true. After working hard without the aid of a label or manager, we found ourselves the living version of this conceptualization. A friend of mine had snapped a photo of us on the massive outdoor stage of

Trent Severn (with guest Tim Timleck and members
Emm Gryner, Dayna Manning, and Lindsay Schindler)
at the Home County Folk Festival.

Victoria Park in London with thousands of people looking on.

Putting the photos next to each other was eerie and astounding. The band has since parted ways, but our high moments were joyful.

THE SPORT OF QUEENS

Making a vision board is not something that most people just wake up and decide to do on their own. Oddly, visualization can be one of the most powerful tools in keeping you on track with your singing practice. On this topic, there is another parallel with the sports world.

In his book *The Psychology of Concentration in Sport Performers: A Cognitive Analysis*, the late Irish writer Aidan P. Moran writes of mental practice, "This idea of a bridge between the phenomenal worlds of intentions and the physical world of actions is paradoxical yet familiar. On one hand, the paradox concerns the possibility that a cognitive process (i.e., mental imagery), which does not involve motor effectors directly, can have a significant impact on motor performance." Moran goes on to say that motor control *is* a cognitive process. We envision whether or not a sofa will fit through a doorway, or we rehearse in our minds a meeting that may be approaching. Although this idea of the mind influencing body, especially in sports, has been debated, Moran points out that the appeal of "mental practice . . . lies mainly in its practical utility as a performance-enhancement strategy for athletes." Moran writes that several star athletes found it quite easy to see and feel "successful key moments" in their minds before they were executed in real life.

In their book, *Applying Sport Psychology*, Jim Taylor and Gregory Scott-Wilson recount the story of celebrated Olympic skiing champion Jean-Claude Killy, who was injured and rendered unable to train. Killy was left with no choice but to prepare by envisioning himself navigating the course to victory, which he did, on this occasion and several times throughout the course of his long career.

In his book *Imagery in Sports and Physical Performance*, writer Anees A. Sheikh describes golfer Jack Nicklaus's insight on the use of visualization for success: "I never hit a shot, not even in practice, without having a very sharp, in-focus picture of it in my head. It's like a color movie." Nicklaus is quoted as saying. "First I 'see' the ball where I want it to finish, nice and white and sitting up high on bright green grass. Then the scene quickly changes and I 'see' the ball going there: its path, trajectory and shape, even its behavior on landing. Then there is sort of a fade-out, and the next scene shows me making the kind of swing that will turn the images into reality." These examples show that with very little effort and expense, we have, at our fingertips, a very real way — a powerful tool — to fast-track our success as singers. **The tool is the mind, and we can decide how to wield it.**

Your vision board — which can be anything from images on a screensaver, a canvas, a scribbled pencil drawing, or a series of words artfully strewn across a page — may not include an image of you singing in front of thousands, or even hundreds. It might not include a shiny award or depict you in a band of singers performing to great adoration and applause. What you imagine is *your vision*, so it can be anything, there are no rules. One singer with whom I worked, named J.P., wanted to record an album his grandchildren would hear, so on his vision board he placed a photo of his family. J.P. made that album, and odds are he'll probably have some grandchildren one day who will hear his collection of songs. Cheryl, another singer whom I worked with, created a vision board only to find that the things she placed on her board — none of which had anything to do with singing and everything to do with her childhood and past self — no longer served her. Able to see her deepest thoughts and feelings in the form of pictures on a board in front of her own eyes, she came to terms with some of her old beliefs. She scrapped the first board and began a new one. The second board embodied her sense of joy, her excitement for the future. She created an image of an old Volkswagen van and cut out pictures of all of her dearest friends (some of whom she made music with) in it, smiling. Cheryl's quest to find her voice brought her to a much different, much deeper discovery because she was able to get visions out of a hidden place and put them somewhere she could stand back and take an objective look at them. Time and time again, I've seen singers' visions come true. An album turns into a real recording, a wish to perform becomes a real concert, a wish to connect with family becomes reality.

Creating a vision for yourself can also be truly joyful. In it, you afford yourself the chance to wipe the slate clean, make a collection of images, words, or feelings that summarize your best self, your future self — the self you've always wanted. When the board is done, I ask my students to put it somewhere they can see it every day. Like having a destination securely put into a GPS or maps app, suddenly you know where you are going, and you're not just driving around aimlessly.

I make vision boards too. One of my more recent vision boards included a mock cover for a book that I would write about singing. I wrote a proposal for the book, made sure it was as perfect as I could make it, was offered a book deal, and now you are holding that book. Labouring over the design of a mock cover seemed a little silly at the time, but by printing it out and putting it into a frame where I could see it, I felt more serious about my project. My fake book cover gave me the fuel to pick up the phone and tell someone about my idea, which ultimately led to this book. Visualization equals results.

ACTION ITEMS

1. **Create a vision board.** Allow your imagination to run wild. Whatever massive dreams you see for yourself, create images that communicate these dreams. Try not to let reason and circumstance get in the way. Don't censor yourself. If your dream is to perform at Radio City Music Hall, place this vision on your vision board. Nobody needs to see it but you.

2. **Create a deadline as to when this vision board will be complete**, or share your vision board with someone you trust. Remember that you can alter

your board as many times as you wish after completing it.

3. **Put your vision board somewhere you can see it all the time.**

CHAPTER 4

GET A VOCAL COACH

*"The beautiful thing about learning is that no one
can take it away from you."*
— B.B. KING

I remember my first vocal lesson like it was yesterday. I
drove a red Ford Festiva — a car that had no business sporting racing stripes, yet it did — to an industrial cul-de-sac in
London, Ontario, feeling uneasy. I pulled up in front of a grey
unmarked building, parked, and climbed the stairs. Once at
the top, I heard someone singing scales behind a closed door.
I waited outside, shifting nervously, until it was my turn. I
thought about bolting out of there, but before I could, the
scale-maker left, and Mitch Seekins welcomed me in. The
room contained a portable keyboard and a couple of chairs
— nothing else. After a bit of chit-chat, we got down to work.

First, Mitch walked me through a warm-up routine,
which I eventually tried on my own. The warm-up felt about

as comfortable as being attacked by blood-sucking leeches in a bottomless lake. I hated the number of weird noises I had to make in front of this new person. I felt like an idiot, flapping my lips and going up and down scales that, to my ear, sounded horrible.

Okay. Let's stop making these ridiculous sounds, and you show me how to become the pop star I am destined to be, I said to Mitch inside my head. Out loud, I asked, "How long will it all take, you know, to get a good-sounding voice?" And he, in his very matter-of-fact, what's-the-big-deal way, shrugged his shoulders and said, "It'll come." I sighed. It wasn't the answer I wanted.

Mitch was right, and it did come — the power, the vibrato, the confidence, the strong singing tone, and, yes, eventually, the massive gigs. But it took time. Also, it's important to note that even our favourite artists started somewhere. A lot of the early work of very established singers reveal a less refined voice. This is helpful to remember as you work to eliminate the goal of "perfection" from your practice. Going with the flow and trusting that your body will cooperate as it becomes ready takes the pressure off of what can begin a very emotional adventure. Allow the spotlight to shine on the day-to-day learning process and whatever joys pop up along the way. Remember, you are not trying to achieve the perfect voice. **You are not trying to "sing like somebody else."** You are unearthing your unique, strong voice. On that journey, you will encounter some mysteries, but you'll also experience a whole bunch of triumphs, big and small.

FIND YOUR VOCAL COACH

And this brings us to **Secret No. 6: You need a good vocal coach.** The right singing coach is so important. Among other things, the right coach can help you avoid one of the worst pitfalls of singing — damage to your vocal cords that comes from the repetition of bad habits.

Although I met Mitch at age 19, how old you are when you find your vocal coach is not a determining factor in how successful you'll be. The degree to which you thrive doesn't depend on age, experience, or background. Instead, it's about making a decision to focus on and commit to singing, backing it up with the faith that you can make it happen. Famous singers like Sheryl Crow, Leonard Cohen, and Debbie Harry didn't even release their first albums until they were in their thirties, and artists like Willie Nelson, Bonnie Raitt, Sia, and Sharon Jones all saw their biggest successes after age 40.

VOCAL COACH SELECTION PROCESS CHECKLIST

Here's a handy checklist you can use when selecting your amazing new vocal coach!

- ☐ Experience
- ☐ Connection
- ☐ Method
- ☐ Your own goals
- ☐ Challenge

☐ Cost

☐ Your Diligence

Experience

My coach, Mitch, grew up in a farmhouse without electricity a hundred miles northwest of Grande Prairie, Alberta. The nearest pavement was 25 miles away. He grew up a "hillbilly" (his words) and in an effort to escape the brutality of the Canadian winter, which was only exacerbated by an uninsulated home, Mitch's mother would rent an apartment with electricity 50 miles away in Dawson Creek for five months of the year. It was at this apartment, at the tender age of five, that Mitch made a discovery that would change his life. His mother played him an LP by the famous opera singer Mario Lanza. The song that got under little Mitch's skin was "Drink, Drink, Drink," and the sound coming out of the record player floored him. The sound of the human voice presented in this extraordinary new way fused to his heart and would become a life-long obsession.

Fast forward some years later and Mitch was no longer a hillbilly living in the bush of Alberta, but a young man who toured, performing pop, rock, R&B, jazz, and even opera — just like his hero Mario Lanza — in front of audiences across North America and Europe.

Mitch's love for singing became intertwined with a fascination with the mechanics of the human voice. Watching Mitch as he describes a process or a function of singing is like watching a giddy scientist. He explains how the voice works like he is putting an invention together before your very eyes, yet he makes it all sound remarkably simple.

This keen understanding of the physiology of singing is at the root of why Mitch does what he does so well and why he is one of the country's most in-demand, successful vocal coaches. At the root of it all, however, is emotion.

"At a very young age, I fell in love with making sound vocally," he explains. "To me it was all about melody, textures, and the emotion that it can produce. Being able to completely immerse myself in the moment and feeling of a song, and hopefully trigger the same in an audience, was everything to me."

Choosing a coach who has been active as a touring or recording singer can be important as they will draw from experience and not just what they know from studying a book or from their own training. Because Mitch had real-life experience, even performing gigs outside the classical genre, he could enlighten me to the fact that the rules for singing opera also apply to pop, rock, country, hip-hop, and every other genre too.

A strong voice is a strong voice. His approach, implementing techniques from one of the oldest types of singing in the world, works.

In my own teaching, I echo his concept. The idea of using intensive training methods to complement one's work can also be seen in sports, where football players and baseball players have been known to supplement their regular training with classes in boxing, yoga, and ballet. NFL player Steve McLendon, a 310-pound nose tackle, credits ballet with helping him strengthen his knees, ankles, and feet. Boxing champ Vasyl Lomachenko studied Ukrainian dancing and followed that up with gymnastics before going on to become one of the greatest amateur boxers of our time. When we consider aspects outside our line of sight that might make what we do better, we enrich the learning experience. Training with regular warm-ups, learning other people's songs, stretching jaw and facial muscles, and exercising to increase breath capacity, as well as the regular vocal lesson, will all move you towards thriving onstage and in the studio.

Connection

A connection with your teacher is absolutely necessary. As Johan Sundberg wrote in his book *The Science of the Singing Voice*, "the emotional relationship between teacher and pupil has a decisive influence on the result of the voice training. If the atmosphere in the studio is not relaxed, the kind of phonation learned in that studio is not very likely to be relaxed either."

At the risk of likening the vocal coach search to dating, you need to follow your instincts initially and examine how being with your coach makes you feel. Pay attention to the words a vocal coach uses during your first conversations or meetings. What kind of language do they use? Do they ask you specific questions about *your* voice, goals, and experience? Do you feel that they care? Does what they say indicate they're actually listening to you when you respond? Talk to other singers they coach and find out how they have felt as a result of studying with the coach. "Singing is so intimate, there has to be a connection," explains Mitch. "If that connection isn't there, you'll have an issue learning."

At my first lessons, I felt painfully shy. I wasn't sure I'd ever break out of that feeling. Over time, the awkwardness with trilling my lips in my warm-up or stretching my face like I was doing an epic Hollywood horror movie mask rip-off subsided. Soon, I was stretching my face and making noises in front of my coach, completely unfazed. Trust was an essential part of the process for me. Trust that your vocal coach is asking you to do these unusual exercises for a reason. **Singing is physical, so you have to get physical.** See if you can envision yourself being connected to your teacher enough to execute these exercises week after week. This connection with your teacher will absolutely lead to a connection with yourself and your audience.

Method

How your teacher teaches is also very important. There are two aspects to this:

1. the overall delivery of the content — whether it's in person or online, in a group or one-on-one — and
2. the content itself, and how it is rolled out.

Let's look at in-person versus online. By considering online lessons as a method of learning, you are not confined to choosing a local teacher; you have a world of options at your fingertips. Online lessons can even be considered a form of safety in times of isolation or quarantine. Although singing is a physical act that ideally requires in-person one-on-one interaction, a vocal teacher who has taught online for a long time will know how to teach effectively over video. A great teacher's approach and spirit will transcend the displacement of distance learning.

As for one-on-one versus group learning, one-on-one is best because your needs need to come before others'. Sure, you can learn a lot at a choir or ensemble practice about harmonizing and group dynamics and even glean some technical tips, but when focusing on improving your own instrument, it's best to hear your voice first on its own, for a long time. That said, the energy of singing with others is palpable, and in a later chapter, you'll get more affirmation about the amazing benefits of singing with others.

The method a teacher uses to introduce you to exercises is really up to them and to you. If you know if you learn best by ear or by reading, this can be helpful to share with your teacher. If you learn well from visuals over audio, or vice versa, this is also worth discussing in your first conversation instead of talking about it five or six lessons down the road.

Your Own Goals

Go ahead and spare yourself the pitfall of eternal disappointment by admitting that a vocal coach isn't going to do all the work for you. Often, we leave ourselves out of the process of learning, deciding our teacher will guide us without our having to put forth much effort. You, and only you, can throw yourself headlong into your training by committing to being open to learning and doing the work on a regular basis. You can also help yourself immensely by clearly knowing what you want. Don't know exactly what that is? The chapter on visualization will help. To paraphrase the film *Jerry Maguire*, help your teacher to help you.

Challenge

From the time I was five until the age of thirteen, I was challenged by my piano teacher. I may not have liked it, or understood it, but because Miss Fawcett of Forest, Ontario, challenged me — not just to be the best pianist I could be but to weather the storms of her difficult personality — I developed a thick skin. Whenever I'd be met by adversity later in my life, I felt that I already had the tools and know-how to deal with difficult situations and people.

Hopefully your teacher doesn't end up poking you in the shoulder or demanding you take the clip-in feathers (trendy in 1984) "out of your hair this instant!" But when it comes to learning anything, we could all use a little push. If your teacher isn't inspiring you and keeping you accountable, ask them to be a little more persistent. If they are willing to be an accountability partner for you, that is, someone who more intensively checks and measures your progress week-to-week, let them. If not, find another teacher who will, or seek out an accountability partner in your life who will push you towards regular practice and healthy habits — a friend, a family member, a bandmate. Tip: Make sure this person is someone you admire and respect and one whose company you enjoy, or nine times out of ten they will fail to be useful as an accountability partner.

Why do we need this? Most of us, though not all, need to be accountable to something or someone other than ourselves; that's just the nature of being human. If we borrow a musical instrument from a friend, we're usually more careful with it than we would be if it were our own.

If another human or your teacher can't be this accountability partner, you can create the same opportunities by setting fixed deadlines. You can create your own deadlines by planning an online or in-person performance or by setting a date in the future that you'll give someone a gift featuring you singing (an audio or video recording). Alarms, calendars, and digital reminders are all ways to stay accountable if you'd prefer to steer clear of all humans except yourself.

Cost

We spend countless dollars on outfits, shoes, makeup, and frivolous household items like bread cutters that cut our kids' sandwiches into the shape of two dolphins spooning, yet we balk at spending money on any kind of music lessons or education. Truth: we are a materialistic society, and sometimes we spend and acquire stuff as a way to feel happy or distracted, or just to have more stuff. But there is hope. Once you remember how much joy singing brings you and once you start seeing results in your voice, you'll start to see the value in the lessons themselves. Budget for singing lessons. If you need to create the space in your budget for lessons, eliminate spending on something that doesn't serve you. How do you determine what doesn't serve you? Take a look at your monthly spending or just open up your online banking statement. Determine exactly where some of your recreational spending takes place. Ask yourself what the circumstances were around that spending. Were you rewarding yourself for something? Were you bored or feeling low? If that spending wasn't part of a bigger plan to nurture habits that make you shine or make you feel good long-term, it may have been part of an unhealthy emotional response. Ask yourself where you can cut back to make room for more good: A homemade coffee instead of a trip through the café drive-thru. A reworking of your existing wardrobe after a bit of research instead of buying something you don't need. A bottle or two less of wine a month. These are just suggestions of places to cut back in exchange for a lesson or something that promotes health.

Many singers also give up if results don't come quickly, and the cost of lessons becomes the hook on which the student hangs their excuses — why the whole idea was crappy in the first place. We also avoid spending money on things like training and education because that very exchange of money for knowledge holds *us* accountable to making it all worthwhile. Sometimes we associate money with our fear of the unknown and, sometimes, as crazy as it sounds, a fear of success (and all the unknowns that come with it). This can lead to pulling the plug on everything.

It's true. Money, our relationship to it, and the way we view it can be complicated. There are many books and resources out there that can help repair your relationship to money if need be. I've included a list of some key ones at the end of this book.

Yes, money is important, but it can also be as confusing and charged a topic as politics, sex, and religion. We were taught things about money in our childhood that influence what we do with it in our adult years. There go those adults, ruining everything *again*. Some common unhealthy thoughts about money that many people have adopted from their early days include "nobody has enough of it," "if you want it or need it, there's something wrong with you," "money is so sacred that it can never be borrowed or given," and my personal favourite money attitude from yesteryear, "don't piss it down a goddamned rat-hole."

If you have hang-ups about money that prevent you from making it, giving it freely, or putting it into something that you know will change your life, look into ways to change your relationship with money. Very late in life, I changed my relationship with money. I began to cherish it, I thought about it in a positive light, and I started to have fun keeping track of it. Rather than being afraid of money or frightened of never having it or thinking it was evil, I started to believe that I could treat it well and it could treat me well too. Adopting this mindset helped my business and allowed me to channel funds into paying my team, taking courses, reading books, doing fitness training, starting new business ventures, and exploring ways to be healthier — all of which helped move me toward achieving my dreams and goals. More importantly, I noticed the more money I made, the more I could give back to others. I upped the quality of my coaching by getting accredited, I demanded higher pay at my gigs, and what I am able to return is of better quality.

In his simple yet powerful book *The Science of Getting Rich*, Wallace D. Wattles emphasizes that you can have more powerful influence by having a positive relationship with money. Instead of looking at money as *going out* towards any given initiative, see it as a fantastic exchange with the universe that will put you on a path of transformation, generosity, and healing.

Like any relationship, however, if it's gotten toxic, it needs healing, and this issue of addressing your relationship with money might be a hard pill for you to swallow. But remember, before you reach for that bookmark and head to the mall, it's 66 days to change a habit. That's not long if you know you'll emerge with a new attitude that could bring you lifelong joy.

Your Diligence

The singers with whom I work with who have the most success are the ones that put in the work. During the week, they do their vocal exercises and make other healthy decisions like maintaining a fitness schedule or participating in an outdoor sport. The lesson becomes more of a "check-in" on their progress, not the most important part of their work. During your lesson, you can tweak a few difficulties or problems, but you'll make a huge leap forward only if you've worked on your own at home. If the lesson is the only time you are putting in effort, your progress will be pretty slow.

Practice doesn't have to be rigid. This is music, not air traffic control at Chicago O'Hare. **Consistency wins in the**

end, and so does seeing the joy in it. As I wrote earlier, you can warm up and sing while you are doing other things. In fact, you may even be more apt to do your warm-up if you build it into existing activities.

ACTION ITEMS

1. **Explore.** Open your eyes and ears to discover who teaches singing near you, or probe around online to learn more about vocal coaches.

2. **Make an appointment.** Once you feel you might have a connection with a teacher, make an appointment to talk on the phone, over video chat, or in person.

3. **Let that vocal coach know who you are and what you need.** Once you start to study, let your vocal coach in. Tell her how you learn best and what you require to thrive in a learning environment.

4. **Create accountability.** Find someone in your life who can keep you on track with your singing, your exercises, and your studying. If no one is available for this role, find three other ways to be accountable to yourself — set alarms, create a calendar, reward yourself for practising.

5. **Step back and take a look at your relationship with money.** In her book *You Are a Badass at Making Money* (which you should read), Jen Sincero suggests that readers write a letter to money. This is an incredibly effective way to discover how your

beliefs about money are holding you back in life. Once you write your letter, read it and see where you can improve. What negatives can you turn into positives?

CHAPTER 5

BE PREPARED

"Small, deliberate actions inspired by
your true desires create a life you love."
— DANIELLE LAPORTE

Although my career would eventually take off, it took work and the work happened early. When I think back, I recall that no one was racing to sign me after hearing the demos I made when I was 16. Still in high school, I was faced with the dilemma of choosing what I wanted to do with the rest of my life. I weighed two options: go to Ryerson University and get a degree in Journalism or take Music Industry Arts at Fanshawe. Ultimately, I chose the music program because no other potential job could compete with my rabid love for music. Making music was such an escape, and I was kind of awestruck that making music and recording in the studio were actual college-credited activities in which you could get a diploma.

My brother Frank had already taken Music Industry Arts (M.I.A. as we called it) and had come out of it somewhat of a legend, landing a job right after graduation as an assistant recording engineer at a studio in Burbank, California. Three years older than I am, he was always blazing his own trail; it was exhilarating to see and eventually follow in his footsteps. During his first years in Burbank, I flew down, and Frank and I did some of our own recording. We always loved getting together and brainstorming musical ideas. Frank was always a mentor of sorts to me, and after glimpsing his life in LA, experiencing a real studio, surrounding myself with palm trees, sunshine, and dreams of a record deal, I was even more pumped about a career in music.

During college, I was laser-focused on songwriting and recording. There were long stretches spent alone in rented apartments absorbing the wonder of Joni Mitchell's *Blue* and Tori Amos's *Little Earthquakes*. The flair these amazing musical women had for saying what they wanted without conforming to norms was inspirational. Sarah McLachlan's *Fumbling Towards Ecstasy* was also on heavy rotation, and during this time in college, I explored life on my own while completely nerding out about recording, playing bass, and dreaming about a pop music career. Visualization was taking place without my even knowing it; I knew there had to be something greater out there for me, beyond the college recording studio and the homemade songs.

FIRST SHOWS

After graduation, I had my eyes on Toronto as a place to start playing concerts. A two-hour drive from my college, the city of four million people was a logical next step. I cut my hair into a jagged, messy 1990s bob, changed my first name from Mary to Emm (I thought Emm sounded androgynous and cool, plus I always thought *Mary Gryner* sounded like someone was chewing on a piece of old beef jerky from underneath their car seat), packed up my music stuff, and left for the big city.

Suspecting that I should surround myself with others who were on the same page as I was, I kept within arms' reach of a handful of musicians from M.I.A. who had also moved to Toronto. A few of these folks become my first band and recording team.

I latched on to a fellow named Stuart Brawley. Stu was undoubtedly the David Foster of the M.I.A. program and probably even owned a few deeply uncool sweaters like the ones Foster used to wear in the '80s. Stu was skilled at coming up with vocal harmonies and even more masterful behind the mixing console. He made recordings sound like butter — deliciously warm, with perfectly placed synth pads, exquisitely pleasing harmonies that sustained for days, and lots of great beats. He had a juicy pop sensibility. Stu had landed a job working at a jingle house in Toronto — a company that recorded expensive TV and radio commercials. After business hours, he and I would sneak in and make our own recordings. By then, I had written many more songs — one called "July," a big-chorused angsty pop song about falling in love with a record producer, and one called "Wisdom Bus," a jam about being completely bewildered by the imbalances of the world.

At night I played in small clubs, donning gold lamé dresses and lots of eyeliner; rocking the piano, guitar, and bass; and singing my heart out. Knowing no one would come to a show by an unknown girl, I phoned up all my M.I.A. friends and invited them to come see me play. My hope was that it would appear to any random big city onlookers that I had a pretty bitchin' following.

One night, when I was playing a cozy club called C'est What, I put into action an early exercise of "fake it till you make it." Before my show, I asked one of my friends if he could shout out a song request for Blondie's "One Way or Another" towards the end of my show. The plan was that, under stage lights and amidst the applause of all my adoring "fans," the band and I would magically be able to field this spontaneous pop-punk request, and everyone would enter a state of bliss they had not been in for dozens of years.

Come showtime, the night went as designed. I played one of my first sets to a room full of actual humans. The humans applauded. We, the band, played well and had a great time. We finished the set, and my friend yelled "Play Blondie!" Although the applause was weakening with every passing second, the band and I returned to the stage from the broom closet, pretending to be big stars that might just have one more in them if the crowd was lucky. In what looked like a display of jaw-dropping impulsiveness, we launched right into the song like we had the entire Top 40 up our sleeves. In hindsight, I realize that the whole audience probably knew that the moment had been planned. And as for the random big city onlookers? They were probably just chatting over their wheat-infused raspberry craft beer, wondering if my concert was someone's private birthday party. All the same, it was part of building a story.

CRAZY DAY JOBS

In order to survive, I took day jobs. Thanks to the muscles I flexed by growing up with a newspaper being made in my basement, I was poised and ready to pounce on any job that afforded me the chance to use a three-hole punch and a photocopier. Luckily for me, office administration jobs for 20-year-olds with no genuine interest in doing anything in an office were plentiful in 1997 Toronto.

My first job was that of a data transcription coordinator for a company that made programs for phones . . . "Press one for . . . Press two for . . ." You know. Taking this job allowed me to pay my rent on a crappy east-end apartment that I shared with a five-foot-tall goth metalhead named Kevin. Every day, I sat in my cubicle, typing out data, quietly observing how the established project managers worked and held themselves. The company grew and grew until we moved into a shiny new building in the dynamic King Street West neighbourhood. Instead of dealing with the daily grind of the nine-to-five, we were soon being whisked upstairs to the top level of the building, a big open concept space for "vision and values" sessions led by perfectly groomed execs in track pants drinking green juice. Feeling a bit like Yoda at New York Fashion Week, I quit to look for other jobs.

I took one job where I was a receptionist for a financial advisor. And then there was my favourite, where I was an accidental graphic designer for a company that heralded one of the most ingenious ideas of the millennium: CDs laser-cut into different shapes.

Always having my eye on the bigger prize of quitting these jobs and becoming a rock star, I kept my music work a secret from almost all of my employers. When a couple named Duane and Trudy hired me as a graphic designer, it was certainly a clerical error (I had never listed graphic design on my resumé), but I figured I knew how to drop clip art into Microsoft Word, so I'd just take the job and hope for the best.

Every morning, Trudy would clip-clop into the office carrying a grande Starbucks coffee in one hand and a Gucci purse in the other, which seemed to me, even in my naïveté, suspicious accessories for someone running a company that cuts CDs into shapes. Duane seemed about eight feet tall. He had big curly hair that went past the nape of his neck and resembled one of Louis XIV's powdered wigs. The husband and wife would sail into work each morning in their Porsche, Duane's pudgy hands adorned with big school rings that caught the office lights just so. But how can he drive a Porsche when he works at a CD shape company? I asked myself, as I waited for the photocopier to warm up and deafen me with its bulldozeresque motor.

I could never quite bring myself to dress business casual. One day, Trudy looked me over and with as much disgust as she could muster, told me to "get a hair brush." I was flabbergasted. I have a hairbrush! I said to myself. But young and easily offended, I looked at myself later that day in the bathroom mirror, gently patting down my choppy 'do with a few drops of tap water. Maybe Trudy was right. Had I spent too much time writing songs and not enough time grooming? Did hoity-toity Trudy, with her pencil skirts and dyed hair slicked back into a bun, have any idea what was trending on Queen Street West? Like, whatever.

Life got worse at the CD shape company, which bore the self-important name Allegiance Entertainment. Duane and Trudy manufactured some promotional CDs in the shape of the letter A to draw attention to their company name, no doubt an idea that had been birthed on some rip-roarin' car ride through the picturesque hills of Caledon. I was part of the team that packed these CDs into padded envelopes and sent them out to the business executives of Toronto.

Shortly after the A CD was mailed out, a very angry man phoned in to complain that one had become permanently lodged in his Lexus's CD player. Oh no, I lamented to myself amid the office panic. The sharp pointy points of the A must have gotten stuck on something in there! I wondered whether maybe, just maybe, the shaped CD was an object that humanity did not actually require.

Office day-job life continued to get weirder. Strange phone calls began to trickle in. There were mysterious voices with weird requests and people hanging up without warning. And then it happened. In a moment that could have easily been a scene from a marginal horror movie circa 1997, death threats began to come through on the office fax machine. They were directed towards my big-haired boss Duane, and the atmosphere in the office went from peculiar to chilling. What had he done to garner this kind of abuse? I wondered. Was the capital A jamming in luxury sedans all across the province? Should they have manufactured a CD in the shape of an O? What kind of terror would have ensued had they manufactured the letter X? Whatever the case, I was barely 20 and I feared only for my own welfare. I wondered silently, If this company tanks, where will I print my concert posters? How will I continue to make personal phone calls during the daytime that forward my music career? Alas, the cell phone had not yet been invented.

After one of the receptionists and I shared a few whispery conversations, it was revealed that my boss had been involved in shady dealings in Europe. I heard something about fraud and "smuggling illegal hair growth products into Spain." Seeing as Duane had more hair on his head than ten Robespierres put together, I decided the claims were probably legit. Between the unnerving scrawl of a would-be killer sputtering out of the fax machine in broad daylight and the sudden implication of illegal activity in beautiful, picturesque Spain, I made the difficult decision to get the hell out of there. In the autumn of 1997, I did what people joke about to musicians all the time — I quit my day job.

GETTING PEOPLE'S ATTENTION

During this whole time of working day jobs, my paycheques had gone to funding my music. With my hard-earned money, I paid for posters, cassette and CD production, outfits, and musical equipment. I had also been passing around my demo CD, which contained songs I had recorded with Frank and Stu. The songs from this time showcased my very

untrained, improper way of singing, but the album had passion, decent songs, and drums that sounded like they had
been recorded with the same enthusiasm as one would have
had making a Toto album.

I didn't know it, but those days in Toronto were my baby
years. I certainly did not need a manager at that stage in
my life, but ego and excitement were ruling me and fueling
me. Knowing how glam and accomplished it would look if I
could say I had my very own manager, I began the search for
one. I figured a manager could also lead me to a record deal,
and a record deal would lead me to being Madonna.

Toronto was exciting to me. What some girls from the
backwoods might find overwhelming, I found invigorating.
The music scene was bustling and supportive. I was ready
to eat it all up. But I drew from some of the expertise of
Terry McManus who once said, "Before you start to sing,
you need to get people's attention."

Terry had told us in class, "A lot of artists started off their
career with some kind of outrageous or novelty look. Think
of the Beatles with their hair or k.d. lang and her suits. And
today is no different . . . you have people adopting outrageous or different looks in order to be noticed . . . and *then*
they sing." In the course of the same lecture, Terry had stood
on the desk in front of the class and talked about how he
could make the class remember him or his lectures. He said
with one of those big smiles on his face, "If I do this lecture
up here, you would not forget that image!"

Terry's words echoed in my head. I knew I had to stand
out. When I could have secured instant fame by taking off
all my clothes and riding a donkey down Yonge Street or

running through Lake Shore Boulevard traffic with nothing but parachute pants and a hot dog on my head, my preferred method of standing out was to send fruit baskets to all the managers in Toronto, along with my music. Yup. Fruit baskets equal wild and crazy. That was just me, though, and throughout this book, I'll encourage you to be you and do things *your* way too.

Carefully, I selected the best, most colourful fruit from the finest grocery store in Toronto, arranged it lovingly in a wicker basket, and wrapped my CD inside. I sealed the arrangement up with cellophane and ribbon and attached the nicest letters, one to each of the greatest music managers in the city. Off I went delivering fruit baskets.

And then I waited.

And waited.

One response came back: "Thank you for your music. It's not my cup of tea, but I ate all the fruit." Others just didn't reply at all. I started to wonder if getting a manager was not going to be as sweet as I thought. Maybe I'd have to streak across the highway after all. As time went on, I felt sick. The lack of interest, which I translated into rejection, was starting to get me down. But finally one day, after much waiting around, a manager returned my call and we made arrangements to meet at a café in the east end, where the peace and grandeur of Lake Ontario met the bustling pavement.

Michael Murphy was an Irishman in Toronto. He was tall, ginger-haired, with wide blue eyes and a wit faster than a fighter jet. When we met, I paid very close attention to the words he used and the way he held himself. He was married to a vibrant MuchMusic VJ named Jana Lynne White, and he referenced her a lot throughout the conversation, showing that her influence on him was important. He then called my music "inspiring." He seemed to know absolutely everyone in Toronto. Feeling satisfied with these little clues about his character and potential, I hired Michael, and we set to work.

———

The day I quit my day job was one I'll never forget. Fear took over my entire body, as I suddenly had no way of making money and no security. I sat across from Michael, who had already been working with me for a few months by that point, feeling lost and daunted by the idea of throwing all of my eggs into the music business basket. Tears filled my eyes. My balls-out 22-year-old cockiness was starting to fade. I felt like a leaf in the wind, swayed by any old thing anyone would say. I remember looking at Michael through tears that day. I am sure the look on my face said it all: "What do we do now?"

THE FIRST BIG WIN

Michael and I hatched plans in more cafés and dreamed up great musical accomplishments. I continued to slug it out in clubs in Toronto once every month or so. I sent my song "Wisdom Bus" to Radio Star, which took submissions of new songs by new artists. The tide turned when, much to my surprise, I won first place in this national songwriting contest.

With the $5,000 Radio Star prize money, I recorded an album I called *The Original Leap Year*. Although I was still sneaking into other studios to record, I could finally pay musicians and everyone working on the album. *The Original Leap Year* was a mix of indie rock and pop inspired by British bands and Tori Amos. Having Michael on board at this time jived perfectly with my youthful ego; he took the music I made, passed it around, and introduced me to everyone and anyone in the Toronto music scene. Suddenly, people were getting to know me — club owners, journalists, record shop owners. Some music publishers and video directors took notice of me, and I met other musicians who weren't just slugging it out in clubs. These people had record deals and were touring. Michael possessed a magnetism and the way he attracted people in the scene had now spilled over into my world. People began to know my name.

My singing on *The Original Leap Year* showed early signs of depth, even though I still didn't know what the heck I was doing. I was studying with Mitch, but I had yet to learn how to breathe low, bring my voice forward, and use my source of power. There were moments when it would show up, and these glimmers of hope gave me motivation. Other times, I would struggle to be heard at my live show over the din of drums and distorted guitars. More often than not, I was rolling the dice on whether or not I'd make it through a show. But my passion for music and a desire for self-expression balanced out the roughness in my singing. Perhaps I was also compelled to go forth thanks to blind faith and lofty goals of fame and fortune. Somewhere in me, I knew I just had to get better at everything — singing, songwriting, networking — and without a real blueprint, I naively decided that if I put my mind to it, I probably would.

When it came time to release *The Original Leap Year*, I hired a publicist named Ingrid Hamilton. For a few hundred dollars, she got me reviews and write-ups in magazines and newspapers. It was this small move — hiring Ingrid the publicist — that propelled me forward in ways I would never have dreamed.

Warren Bruleigh, who had produced the Violent Femmes, read one of the write-ups about my album in a magazine. Intrigued, he got a hold of it and passed it on to a record exec in LA. After a few meetings with this exec and casually considering a few other labels' offers, I signed a worldwide record deal with Mercury Records. Soon, I was off to London, England, to record my dream album that would be heard by everyone all over the world.

Luck played a big role in the success of winning the contest and getting the record deal, but **I prefer to see luck as favouring those who put themselves in the path of opportunity.** Travel, meeting people, entering contests, sending fruit baskets, taking the jobs, quitting the jobs, all of these things — geeky or not — were examples of preparedness. I prepared myself to enter the music business, not knowing if I actually belonged there or not.

John Hazen, a sound technician friend of mine who spends enormous amounts of time setting up, ringing out a room, and testing audio equipment before he mixes a show, often says to me he is just "setting the conditions for success." In Toronto in the late 1990s, I was doing the same. My choices made it easier for others, people like Michael, the publicist, Warren, and Mercury Records, to find me. My work of creating stability, working on my voice, constantly songwriting, recording, playing live, and meeting people made it easier for success to take place. Although it's true we can't control life, we can make it easier for luck and opportunity to find us. Which brings us to **Secret No. 7: Set the conditions for success.**

My dad always said, "You have to be prepared to do everything you need to do to make your dreams come true. You may not have to do these things, but you have to be prepared to." And beneath that preparedness is something even more important: your *why*.

ACTION ITEMS

1. **Write down three things you can do today to forward one of your goals or visions.** These can be big or small, but make sure they can be executed. For example, my goals back in the day were 1) find a day job so I could pay my rent while I worked on music, 2) put together a band and play in front of an audience — any audience, and 3) find a manager.

2. **Visualize.** Divide a piece of paper into three sections. On the bottom, write your current situation, and on the top third, write what you envision your life as a singer to be. What does it look like? Leave the middle blank for the universe to do its work. Yes. I really wrote that. And it really works.

CHAPTER 6

THE WARM-UP

"Words mean more than what is set down on paper. It takes the human voice to infuse them with deeper meaning."
— MAYA ANGELOU

Stretches, lip trills, scales — up and down — it all sounds dreadfully off-putting. But it's the warm-up routine, its brief, consistent action — one I've taken before every singing event, speaking engagement, radio show, or important meeting — that is a key thing you can do to treat your voice well.

What is the warm-up? **The warm-up is a physical action that allows blood circulation to increase in the vocal cords.** Quite simply, the vocal warm-up is a series of exercises designed to loosen the muscles you use when you sing. These exercises help to eliminate mucus and reduce the risk of wearing yourself out, which can lead to injury.

Whether it's been before taking to the stage at Wembley Stadium for NetAid, singing to hospital workers from my living room, or giving a talk to a university class, warm-ups have not only elevated my ability as a singer, they change my state of mind, and doing them will probably change yours. Consider your warm-ups a "coming out of your shell" or "bringing your instrument forward." When you warm up, you move your voice closer to the audience. You bring your music out from its deepest place, and you allow for a stronger connection with what you're saying and what you're feeling. If expression is our ultimate goal as singers, warm-ups make that all-important target so much easier to hit.

The times when life gets the best of me and I have either forgotten my warm-up or rushed it, I notice I'm less prepared for performing. I'm less expressive, less confident, and my voice sounds thin. Years ago, I occasionally used to lose my voice in concert. Today, because of my desire to have successful performances and experiences, the warm-up has become a non-negotiable part of my practice.

Warming up, however, is different for everyone. Before taking to the stage, Bowie wouldn't warm up as much as he'd bellow out one or two notes, somewhere up towards the high end of his register. Mark Plati, who spent a lot of time in the studio with David as his producer and fellow musician, says that Bowie would just croon out "those high notes" before singing. "[It was like] blowing out the cobwebs. No scales or other exercises." I often wondered how this was enough for David, but it was still a warm-up — one that worked for him. In addition to this, he prepared in all kinds of other ways behind the closed door of his dressing room. One of his rider stipulations during our time together was to have two local newspapers on hand. Did this act of getting the news help David become more connected to the audience he was about to perform for? Maybe.

Consider the warm-up — however big or small a part of your routine you make it, and whatever else you do to prepare alongside that warm-up — a bridge between you and the audience. Time alone before you sing or having a laugh with your bandmates or choirmates can also be helpful. You may have a makeup routine, a yoga routine, visualization techniques, or power poses. Drummers roll sticks on practice pads before they go on, guitar players grab a guitar and noodle backstage before a show. Phil Collen of Def Leppard downs a vegan smoothie and kickboxes for an hour before going on. Just as the entire act of singing is individual to you, your pre-show, pre-studio routines will be uniquely you. For Bowie, a note or two. For me, 20 minutes of warming up. Find what works for you. But whatever you decide, remember **Secret No. 8: Warm up!**

Your vocal coach should have some type of a warm-up routine for you. Sometimes it's helpful if they create a guide track or a video that you can follow along with in times outside of the lesson. I have created a few warm-ups in different registers that you can follow at emmgryner.com.

SAMPLE WARM-UP

The first exercise you do might comprise the following:

1. Belly breathing (no sound yet)
2. Facial and body stretches (no sound yet)
3. Lip or tongue trills (sound)

4. Chest voice exercises (chest voice is the commonly used register for singing most pop/rock songs)
5. Head voice or falsetto exercises (head voice and falsetto are our more "operatic" sound)
6. Lip trills to end
7. Any other stretches (no sound)

In her legendary book *Bel Canto: A Theoretical and Practical Vocal Method*, the famed German mezzo-soprano Mathilde Marchesi wrote that short, simple practice is more effective for long-term gain than long, gruelling warm-up routines. For beginners, she suggests no more than five minutes' warm-up at a time. This should come as amazing news for anyone who thinks they have to be warming up for hours on end every day to see progress. Paradoxically, Marchesi argued that the voice can't be developed in a year or two necessarily, that it takes more of a deliberate, slow pace of short, accurate practice to see results. Sometimes those results show in six months, sometimes two years, sometimes five.

RELAX, JUST DO IT

One of the most important preparations for a warm-up is relaxation. Although you need to treat singing like a sport, you won't be able to flex any muscles or train seriously without being ultra-relaxed. This is **Secret No. 9: Relax, just do it.**

When stress exists in the body, we can go into fight or flight mode, which, as it relates to singing, can affect your ability to use your muscles properly. Stress can result in dry mouth or throat, neither of which is great for singing. Diving even deeper, there exists a lot of research about psychogenic voice disorders that can result in complete voice loss due to emotional factors, or emotional factors caused by a vocal injury or other medical problems. But more often than not, the causes of blocks in the voice are simpler, as Calgary-based speech-language pathologist Sandra Merzib explained to me for this book:

> Stress can definitely have a negative impact on a person's voice. For example, if a person who is regularly using their voice is also stressed out, they are less likely to be focusing on good vocal hygiene or properly taking care of their voice. They are less likely to maintain good vocal habits such as vocal rest as needed, hydration, and understanding and respecting the limits of their voice. They might be prone to indulging in potentially negative habits such as smoking; drinking excessive amounts of caffeine or alcohol; talking in a lower than habitual pitch due to fatigue, resulting in a gravelly voice; holding tension in the chest, shoulders, and throat (resulting in a strained vocal quality); and not resting their voice when they are sick or overly fatigued. The constant strain this places on the vocal mechanisms can lead to aphonia without the presence of anything like lesions, nodules, or polyps to explain why this might be happening. It can also lead to nodules, cysts, or lesions on the vocal folds, which will negatively impact voice

quality. It can be a bit of a vicious cycle at that point — stress has a negative effect on the voice, then the resulting vocal damage is now a source of stress, and so on.

Stress and how to alleviate it deserves its own book. We have been inundated for years with various ways we can relieve stress, and sometimes that overload of information is stressful in itself. What calms one person might agitate another, so there's no blanket list for what will allow you to explore relaxation perfectly. However, as it relates to singing, and in my experience as a coach and performer, I've seen a couple of commonalities on the road to relaxation. As you might guess, the following tips are equally mental and physical, and you'll find yourself best able to reap their rewards when you use them together.

Adjust your expectations. This is easier said than done, but still worth moving towards. Have you ever witnessed someone you admire screw up onstage? He or she might laugh or act awkwardly, the audience may laugh with them, and sometimes there's a gesture of applause and acceptance. At times like these, we see in the object of our admiration our own flaws. We loosen expectations on them and ourselves. We can breathe more deeply. We know we are not alone in our imperfection. The same approach can be applied to the warm-up. Don't expect perfection. Just sing.

Practise deep breathing. Diaphragmatic or belly breathing, which I encourage my students to do for at least two minutes before warming up, makes such a major difference when it comes to performance. Even if a singer hasn't mastered this, deep breathing allows the body and mind to relax and makes way for a fuller voice.

This combination of relaxing and deep breathing is a great starting point for seeing success in your warm-up, singing in general, and most of life as well. But don't forget to *do*. The warm-up routine is something you'll need to put this book down to dive into. It can't be taught through reading. Again, for a quick start, visit my site and watch my intro warm-up video. It's free for you to watch as many times as you need.

ACTION ITEMS

1. **Make a list of three times you were really, truly relaxed.** What were the surrounding circumstances? Can you draw from those moments of relaxation? What helped you get there?

2. **Schedule some time just for relaxing and singing.** Maybe you are going for a drive and sing in the car. Maybe you are going to try belly breathing and some warm-ups. Whatever you decide, schedule it. Then relax.

3. **Try for consistency.** It's easy to start these practices and then lose steam. Whatever it takes for you to stay consistent, whether it's an accountability partner, an entry in your calendar, or an alarm, make it happen. Consistency doesn't mean doing it every day and beating yourself up if you miss one. It's about starting and getting back to it if you get off track. See it all happening for

yourself and remember what you have to do to make warm-ups, relaxation, and singing a priority in your life.

Part 2

LIVING AS
A SINGER

CHAPTER 7

GET OUT THERE

"Art isn't art without an audience."
— DAVID BOWIE

Before my record deal, I said yes to everything: I sang in folk cafés and dive bars. I played bad '90s songs at battles of the bands. I listened to all kinds of music, from Carole King to The Clash, the Sugarcubes to the Pixies. After recording my album for Mercury, I continued to say yes to almost every performance opportunity. I got invited to tour across the US and Canada with guitarist Bernard Butler, formerly of the band Suede. Ron Sexsmith and I toured across Canada. His band and I jammed ourselves into a cargo van to meander through our nation's vast landscape as Canadian musicians do. There was even a day when a college rep at Mercury thought I'd fit right in at Serendipity ice cream shop in New York City, going table to table, strumming my acoustic guitar and singing sad songs to kids and families that just wanted to eat ice cream on a sunny day in peace (great idea, college rep!). I played living room shows — singing for fans in their homes all across North America and Europe. I played in legendary clubs like the Troubadour in LA and Club Passim in Cambridge. I played in boardrooms to corporate nine-to-fivers wearing freshly pressed clothes and just as eagerly strummed a few tunes to kids at campus radio stations.

Some of these performances were assigned to me, but most of them were ones I wanted to explore. I wanted to forward my music and to get out there. If I had limited myself to only singing lessons and recording in my basement, I would only have gone so far. Exploring the world made a huge difference to my progress as a singer, so this makes **Secret No. 10: Get out there!**

Live performance, whether it's out in the world, online, on your porch in front of friends, or on a stadium stage, is so important. When we sing and practise at home, we only move forward so far. We need the trial by fire that only playing in front of an audience can bring. **We learn so much more about ourselves when we venture out into the world.** Only outside our comfort zone do we introduce ourselves to adrenaline, nerves, humans, the shifty eyes of the skeptics, and the adoring gazes of people enraptured with our music. Only out in the world can we really come to terms with the new sounds of our voice coming out of a sound system, weather issues, temperature changes, the strangely nerve-wracking phenomenon of playing a show when your mom is sitting in the first row clapping out of time. These are all things that we need to experience in order to know our voices and get better.

So how do you get out there? A few ways:

1. **Look around your community for opportunities to sing.** These could be open mic nights or they could be karaoke events. They may seem trite or amateur, but a live show is a live show, especially at the beginning. Even the smallest one will help you grow. When I was asked to audition for the Broadway production of *Spider-Man: Turn Off the Dark*, I had to sing the classic rock song "White Rabbit" and a song of my choosing, "Bau-Dachöng" by the Virgin Prunes (a cover from my album, *Songs of Love and Death*). I had never performed either of these songs anywhere, so in preparation for the big audition, I trekked down to the Poacher's Arms pub in London, Ontario. Although it was hard to take everything I've learned and all my experience and show up at an open mic night in a low-lit, downstairs pub, I eventually got over myself and picked up that pen to put my name down on the list of people who wanted to sing that night. I sat there, waiting to sing. I felt like I was taking my driver's test. I had to demonstrate my abilities before I could get that licence to do doughnuts in the parking lot. I knew I had to sing these songs in front of humans, any humans; if I didn't, the first place I'd be singing them would be in an audition room in Manhattan to a panel of experts who had seen and heard some of the best singers and actors in the world.

I didn't get the part in Spider-Man, but I did deliver a great audition. Better yet, I went to New

York City, muscles flexed, prepared. And as it turns out, that musical kind of tanked anyway.

2. **Join a choir.** Joining a community choir has so many benefits. You'll engage with your community, you'll meet other people, you'll sing alongside new friends, you'll be accountable to others, and you'll show up. You'll be expected to know your music, and on the day of performance, you'll be asked to present yourself in something other than your pajama pants and Ramones T-shirt. Online choirs exist too. Look hard enough, and you will find niche choirs — little groups of singers who specialize in certain genres. Choosing a solid organization that has regular practices and performances — whether they're online or in person — can be a great way to get out there.

3. **Start something.** Another way to build your singing practice is to simply start a project. Try to start it with someone you know well or trust, so that your goals are aligned. The sky's the limit with this choice because you truly are at liberty to create any type of band, duo, or solo project that you want.

Two young kids named Joe and Andrew went to American DJ Porter Robinson's show and became inspired to start a project themselves. Although they were studying full-time at Western University, they started making music in their dorm room. Soon, they released the track "Body" under the artist name Loud Luxury.

Thousands upon thousands of streams and many awards later, they're a deep house force to be reckoned with and one of the most successful duos of the genre. You never know what a partnership or project can blossom into. Creating a vision board for your project can also help everyone involved stay on track. Regular practices and check-ins are a good idea. Good, regular communication is always super-important.

4. **Book a show for yourself.** Connect with a venue or booking person to lock down your own show. If playing live doesn't sound like a great idea, construct a special online performance. Put your event on the calendar and then work backwards from that date to prepare for the show. If you feel comfortable with the idea, book more than one show around that time. When you're performing this handful of shows, you'll be basking in your own radiant light — the light of experience and pride. You'll be glad you put yourself out there no matter how it goes.

5. **Offer your singing services to someone.** Offer to sing the national anthem at a local event or sports game. Offer to sing a song for someone's birthday or anniversary party — even just one song. Sometimes planning to record a song by a certain date, say as a gift for someone you trust, will help you "get out there."

And remember, sometimes getting out there doesn't mean doing something musical. Sometimes getting out there means travelling, walking in nature, visiting a friend, going to a cabin alone. These moments can give us clarity about our work, our play, and our dreams.

ACTION ITEMS

1. **Take one action towards getting out there.** Look at the list above and see what appeals most to you. If it's travel, book that getaway. If it's looking around your community for places you could sing, make that first step towards finding out more. A phone call. An email. A conversation. Action creates motivation; when we freeze, when we do nothing, that's so much worse than taking even the smallest baby step towards getting out there.

2. Once you've taken one small action, simply **keep going. Follow through with what you've done.** If you sent an email to a choir director, make a plan to show up at a practice. If you figured out the cost of a trip, find a way to start saving for it. If you inquired about booking a show for yourself and you received an answer, take the next step by asking, "How can I secure this?" or "Where else would be a good place for me to play, and how can I make it a reality?"

CHAPTER 8

WHY THE HECK?

"She stood in the storm and when the wind did
not blow her way, she adjusted her sails."
— ELIZABETH EDWARDS

Identifying the reason you want to sing is one of the most important things you can do to see success. Reconnecting with why the heck you do anything like singing or creating music can be like a heart-to-heart with a friend, where you get to air your deepest feelings on things, and in return, you are heard and supported. Sometimes when I work with my coaching clients, the tasks at hand can become the focus — productivity, increasing income, accountability, staying creative, and so on. Sometimes I just have to stop and rewind things and ask my clients why they do what they do at all. The answers are always riveting. "It's the only time I feel alive." "It's the only thing that matters to me." "Making music is when I am 100 percent happy." These statements remind my clients why they're doing all of the work they're doing. Despite the weight of these answers, each of us is human and we sometimes get so busy *doing* that we forget these ever-important mottos and mantras.

If I didn't know *my* why, I would not have been able to endure this charming list of events:

1. A fan threatening to slit my throat and blow up a building in New York.
2. The government auditing me and insisting I pay tens of thousands of dollars that I didn't have.
3. People saying my record label was fake.
4. A *Globe and Mail* review of one of my concerts in which it was written that I dressed like a teen hooker.
5. My major label dropping me within a year and half of signing me.
6. Babies shooting out of my vagina and taking up all my time.
7. Divorce.

I'll discuss in more detail how singing got me through difficult times. But first: a story.

NOT A GOOD TIME TO BE IN A ROCK BAND

At age 21, a worldwide record deal in my back pocket, I was living the high life. Bestowed upon me were thousands upon thousands of dollars, a crazy big recording budget, and the chance to record my dream album at the legendary Maison Rouge studio in London, England. Limos were coming around for no apparent reason, and I appeared in teen magazines like *Seventeen* and industry papers like the *Hollywood Reporter*. With the big advance I got from the label, I bought my family nice gifts like plane tickets for trips across the ocean. I bought my first car. I was the talk of the town. Even getting a small paragraph in *Bass Player* magazine felt as though someone had placed a jewel-encrusted crown on my head and told me I was ruler of the free world. Just like I planned, my little-girl dreams — from the geeky to the gigantic — had come true.

But the good times were not to last.

On December 21, 1998, the *New York Times* trumpeted the headline: "A Major Merger Shakes Up the World of Rock." The article began with, "Right now is not a good time to be in a rock band." Just a year after I had signed my deal, Mercury Records' parent company, Polygram, was swallowed up in a $10.4 billion acquisition by Seagram's. In what seemed like the blink of an eye, everything went up in flames — the record deal, the sleek black cars, the tours, the team of 50 people working on my record from high atop a building in Manhattan, and, maybe most sad of all, the enthusiasm and excitement from others in the business about me and my music. Suddenly, even though my record was freshly released, no one could care less.

My A&R woman, Allison Hamamura, was replaced with Jeff Fenster, the chap who had signed Britney Spears. He had one week to decide whether to keep me on the label. He did not, and I was dropped. Thousands upon thousands of other artists were dropped, and hundreds of employees were fired. The only artists who were spared a grisly axe-chopping were people like U2, Sheryl Crow, and Sting. I guess the powers that be figured *they* could sell records. My larger-than-life picture came down from the corridor inside Manhattan's iconic One Worldwide Plaza building. "I wonder who this is," I imagined the workers saying as they dismantled the hardware. Very few people would hear my record. Throughout the Canadian industry, there were rumblings that my career was dead. Condolences trickled into my Hotmail account, and one newspaper trumpeted the headline that "the Change from Major to Minor" had come for me.

If there were feelings of panic and defeat, I buried them. My faith to carry on as a pop star was greater than my desire to simply call it a day. I had met so many wonderful people as a result of being signed, and radio stations were still spinning my summertime hit, "Summerlong." I decided to soak up any buzz that being on the now-defunct label was still generating, pick up the pieces, and look ahead.

I looked at the way I was giving concerts. Since my teen years, I had always played with a full band — distorted guitars, big drum kits, and loud bass. I loved how bombastic these shows could be, how similar to the recordings they sounded. But as many of my performances at that time were promotional (that is, they were mostly for radio stations and media), my approach to playing had changed. I had been taking songs which were layered heavily with instrumentation and playing them acoustically, using only piano or guitar and my voice. I loved playing this new way because it was fresh — the words I wrote were easier to sing and be heard and the emotion seemed to translate better. **Allowing the words to come through helped me connect with my fans.** My voice didn't have to compete with a band when I sang. There was something intimate about it, something empowering. I was a girl getting up there by myself with my songs, my piano, and my guitar. I was an army of one. It was powerful. It was revealing. It was enough and sometimes more than enough. My voice could be heard.

Record deal in the bin, I decided to make a new album in a way that echoed this intimate sound. I rented a cottage in the small lakeside city of Goderich, Ontario. I packed up all of my stuff, including an 8-track minidisc recorder, a recording device that was archaic even for the time, and moved out to Lake Huron for a few weeks, leaving Toronto behind. The budget? Five hundred dollars.

Someone watching from the sidelines may have deemed the whole thing crazy or pathetic. After all, I had just made an expensive, lush album for Mercury with people who had recorded with Radiohead, Talk Talk, and other musical legends. I called this new cottage album *Science Fair* because I viewed the whole thing as a sort of school-age experiment. What can I do on my own? I asked myself. What concoctions can I make with what is left over to me? As it turned out, I could do a lot with a little.

At that moment, I had no idea what the future held — that in less than a year's time, I would go on tour with David Bowie, perform on *Saturday Night Live*, and jet off to Europe. My only goal at the time of moving out to the lake to record another album was just to keep making music and doing my own thing.

Making *Science Fair* was sublime. I was the producer, so I called all the shots. I layered drum beats with harpsichords, asked cellist Kevin Fox (a celebrated Toronto-based multi-instrumentalist with whom I had played live several times) to come out and put some gorgeous strings on tracks. The album was a mix of pop songs and ballads. I wrote about my experiences on tour and the characters I had met along the way. I lost myself in the joy of creating.

Outside Music, the distribution company that had helped me before I was signed, graciously took me back and together we released the album. Since I had the ears of the industry already, the press embraced *Science Fair* with open arms. More importantly, my fans loved it.

After its release, I found myself going back to the distributor to order more and more copies. "Back again?" they'd say at the loading dock. *Science Fair* quickly outsold my major label album. The response was overwhelming. People told me how much they loved the album, that it was a soundtrack to their year, to their college days, to their coming out. I received a handwritten letter from Gord Downie of the Tragically Hip, in which he told me how much he enjoyed the songs and the album. The surprise success of *Science Fair* inspired me to make music on my own label. For the first time in a long time, I could see how things were going to work out. From the ashes of a major label deal gone up in smoke, I rose a little bit wiser, with my voice a little clearer and a spring in my step.

Instinct, determination, and curiosity were all things that led me to this post–*Science Fair* place of rejuvenation and feeling powerful. But underneath those things, unbeknownst to me at the time, was my *why*. Without answering the why of what I was doing, I would just be working hard, going through the motions, shifting my energy from place to place. But knowing why you do what you do — that you are working towards something *for a reason* — gives your pursuit harmony. Although I was still getting to know who Emm was, I can say that my why at the time of all of this change was rooted in a love of creating, a belief in self-expression, and a determination to turn tragedy into triumph.

We all think we know why we do things. We might say, "I sing because it makes me happy." But why does it make you happy? And how do you get really honest with yourself to figure out this *deeper why*? **Secret No. 11: Know your why.**

Your vision board, which should embody your deepest desires about life and music, is where you will find your why. If you've made one, take a good look at it. If you haven't, stop reading, do it, and come back to this chapter. Don't put it off — it's one of the most important things you can do.

My why has evolved over the years and I can say that being more crystal clear about it has made the past few years more lucrative but also more joyful because I possess more trust and knowing that I'm going the right way. No longer a twenty-something trying on a bunch of hats, I can narrow down my desired life to a few important aspects.

My vision board has six photo elements:

1. me standing in front of a large crowd giving a talk
2. strangers laughing
3. my rock band's banner hanging on the stage in

front of thousands of people at Festival d'été de Québec — the biggest outdoor music event in Canada

4. me walking hand in hand with the love of my life
5. a fashionable, powerful woman
6. a microphone in a pile of money

The words *love*, *laughter*, *female power*, and *singing* are also on my vision board. Sure, my vision board is a pretty collage, but what is it saying?

My vision board is championing the following treasures of life:

1. speaking to a crowd = connection and sharing
2. people laughing = humour
3. a huge audience = connection through music
4. me and a partner = love
5. fashionable woman = beauty
6. mic in the money = prosperity and success

I ask myself: Why do these things matter to me? Is it ego? Is it my deep desire to show up the judgey high school kids who thought I would never become anything? No. These images are clues to my deeper passions and my purpose.

Deeper passion and purpose can be found when you go one step further again. Break down why the things that matter to you actually matter to you.

For me, connection and sharing leads to peace in the community; they lead to acceptance of difficult feelings. Humour heals wounds. It allows for escape from our world's troubles. Love equals better health, a supported life, possibility. Beauty represents health. Wellness is a gateway to more meaningful work. Recognition means people will trust me so that I can help change their lives, the way mine has changed. Prosperity and success mean I can give more to others from a place of abundance.

Therefore, my why is this: a deep belief in peace in the community, healing pain, better health, possibility, meaningful work, giving back, and changing lives. And all of this, just because I love to sing and share knowledge. Who knew that strolling around the house, belting out "How Will I Know?" by Whitney Houston in your high-waist underwear might actually mean you're trying to find a way to see change in the world?

The following action items will help you find your why.

ACTION ITEMS

1. **Look at your vision board.** If you haven't made one, go back to Chapter 3 and complete Action Items 1 and 2. (Make your vision board and create a deadline for it).

2. **Write down what each image or word on your vision board really means to you.** It's easy to lose your way, and this board is to encourage you when you're faltering. So ask yourself: What are one or two words you can associate with each image or word? If you have a photo of yourself performing onstage, what is that picture really

depicting? Is it expression? Is it happiness? Is it relief? Is it release? What meaningful things are you doing or imagining yourself doing in each image? List them.

3. Go through the list you just made and **ask yourself two questions about each answer — "What do I believe about this?" and "Why is it important to me?"** Write down your answers in a second list. For example, if you associated *expression* with a photo of performing, write down what you believe about expressing yourself and why it's so important. Your answer might be something like, "Expression helps people feel less alone. This is important to me because when I was younger, I felt alone and wasn't allowed to express myself." Go deep, or go home.

4. **Remember the answers on your list.** They will be your support in hard times. They will remind you of your journey and your hard work. They are associated with your values, your beliefs, and your power.

CHAPTER 9

IF YOU SAY RUN,
I'LL RUN WITH YOU

*"What is art? It is the response of the
man's creative soul to the call of the Real."*
— RABINDRANATH TAGORE

DAVID

People always ask me, "What was Bowie like?" I often answer
this question by saying he was kind. He had a quirky but
deeply intelligent sense of humour, and his curiosity for art
and music was profound. But there was also a kind of magic
that infused the room when he walked in. He was at times
otherworldly, and I believed, at the time I sang with him,
when I was 25 and he was 52, he was in a place of joy. He was
expecting a baby with his wife, Iman, making new music
after the techno-heavy phase of the album *Earthling*, and
could be found kicking around New York with ease in plain
clothes, dark shades, and a canvas bag slung effortlessly over
his shoulder. In the year 2000, although he seemed content,
he was still a natural risk-taker, unpredictable and vital.

My earliest memory of David Bowie, the celebrity, is watching him dance alongside Mick Jagger in the video for "Dancing in the Streets." I would have taken it in, parked in my living room with a bowl of Ritz crackers in my lap, some afternoon after school watching *Video Hits* on the CBC. I already knew his mega-hit "Let's Dance" from hearing it on the radio a zillion times, and what stood out most to me was his ever-changing vocal sounds, and the playful depth his voice would plunge when he bellowed out the line "the serious moonlight!"

Fast forward fifteen years and I was offered the chance to sing backing vocals on an upcoming promo tour. Not knowing much about Bowie, my instincts told me to say yes. Immediately, faced with a mountain of songs to learn, I started to listen to Bowie with brand new ears. Beyond that deep voice that coloured early '80s pop radio, there was a legacy I knew nothing about.

People ask how I became a part of the Bowie band, and all I can say is that it was a product of being in the right place at the right time (which I now call "putting myself in the path of opportunity"). My album *Science Fair* in hand, I had started to play places I wanted to visit as a tourist, including New York. My manager, Michael, had just begun working with an artist named Holly Palmer, and when Holly and I crossed paths at a show, we became fast friends. She recommended me as a backing vocalist for Bowie's band, of which she was already a part. I had never been a backing vocalist before and knew very little about harmonizing while shaking percussion, but having just been released into the indie wilderness after being dropped, I felt free to explore any opportunity that came my way. It was easy to be open. **Secret No. 12: Be open to anything.**

I met David Bowie on September 28, 1999. He waltzed into rehearsal wearing a rust-coloured hoodie and dark glasses, hair freshly straightened, full of what I now know to be his trademark energy, the kind of magic that takes over a room, making everyone put their own actions under the microscope while hoping for an intimate moment with the charismatic legend. "You must be Emm," he said with a smile, and shook my hand. He looked at me intently, and I felt as though I was meeting a gentleman more than a famous person.

The first gig to prepare for was *Saturday Night Live*, but other gigs loomed. That first day we ran through the songs; about one third from his most recent record, a sort of throwback to traditional songwriting called *hours . . .* , and the rest from his enormous back catalogue. "Rebel Rebel," "Always Crashing in the Same Car," "Changes," "Word on a Wing," "China Girl" . . . the list went on. When I wasn't singing my parts (which I had memorized like I was studying for an important school exam), the musician in me stood quietly in the corner, in awe of the band I suddenly found myself in. I quickly saw how invaluable it could be to have the perspective of a "hired gun," especially in the band of a pop icon, as I reflected on my own future as a solo artist.

SURREAL

We performed on *SNL* (which was surreal, seeing as I had spent many Saturday nights in my childhood living room watching the show and memorizing skits) and, not long after, *The Late Show with David Letterman*. Although we'd only known each other a few months — having performed a few times together in and around New York — Holly and I quickly found that we had about a thousand things in common. Neither of us had been on the sets of these popular late-night shows before, so we traded impressions and soon became kindred spirits. We loved running around, exploring the back hallways of these big shows, talking about making music, and sharing our individual dreams. We chased down Molly Shannon backstage at NBC. We once bumped into David Letterman in a back hallway of the TV studio, and, quicker than I've seen a man move, he hightailed it the other way — probably thinking we were audience members gone rogue. We passed out copies of our music to anyone who happened to be interested, all the while loving that we were singing with Bowie. Someone like him could choose anyone in the world to belt out those famous *oh-oh*s in "China Girl" or those classic lines in "Drive-In Saturday"— and we knew it.

The most dramatic shift arrived the week after *SNL*, in the UK. We performed three songs on the English TV show *TFI Friday*, where a live audience sits mere feet away from the stage. The energy of this audience could not be contained, and it was then that I started to realize the magnitude of my new day job. So accustomed to walking onstage and having everyone look at me, I soon realized that I was part of David's multicoloured, ever-changing backdrop. Next came the overwhelming feelings of humility and excitement, and the unforgettable sight of pure bliss on the faces of the enraptured audience members. As everyone broke into wild applause after our first song, David turned to me and Holly, smiled, and shouted, "Welcome to London!"

———

Wembley Stadium was a place I had always dreamed of seeing a concert, so to take part in the NetAid concert was perhaps the most surreal part of our first trip. NetAid was meant to channel the power of the internet to eradicate third-world debt, following in the footsteps of other big concerts like Live Aid. Some pretty big names had dressing rooms down the hall — Annie Lennox, Robbie Williams, Stereophonics — and at one point I sat next to George Michael, admiring his impeccably groomed facial hair and perfect skin. When I went to get a drink from the bar backstage, I hummed along to "Summer of '69," which came over the speakers. People around me laughed thinking I was très uncool, but I wanted to remind them that the singer of that song was actually somewhere in the building. Famous people were at every turn. There was so much to laugh at, and so much at which to marvel.

NetAid was broadcast from three different cities — New Jersey, Geneva, and London — but it was clear that Wembley was the only venue packed to the hilt, where you could see hands in the air for what seemed like miles. The passion in the stadium was immeasurable. I stood in the wings with the rest of the band while David opened the set with a piano-and-vocal version of "Life on Mars?" There it was — that stripping-down of music to an intimate quality that I loved so much, reducing me to a sentimental wreck; this song, which I now consider one of the greatest ever written, would always make me feel exquisitely impaired.

During parts of "China Girl," I could hear my voice stretch out across the expanse of the stadium. I dreamed of coming back one day. Little did I know the historic stadium would be demolished a few years after our performance, to make way for a new modern venue.

———

There were three intimate club shows during our first run. The first was in Dublin, the second in Paris, and the third in Vienna. Dublin was a trip. I remember seeing the Rolling Stones at the Horseshoe Tavern in Toronto in September of 1997 and recalled how inspiring it was to take in a legendary act in a small club. I wondered if some of these people — an audience of all ages —were feeling that same buzz as they experienced David and our show. Later, we all retreated to the after-party, where anyone who was anyone in Dublin seemed to be.

Paris was perhaps my favourite of the club shows. Beth Orton and Ron Sexsmith, two of my songwriting idols, were in the crowd. At the after-party, I witnessed David Bowie meeting Ron Sexsmith. The thought of their combined songwriting talent was explosive. Ron told David that he wished he had played "Can You Hear Me?" — one of Ron's favourites. There are so many songs in David's back catalogue that everyone always wants to hear a different one, which I remember thinking at the time must be a fantastic problem to have.

Later on at the after-party, "Let's Dance" started playing over the speakers. I leaned over to David who was sitting right next to me and told him this was one of the first songs of his I had ever heard. "When were you born?" he asked, flabbergasted. "1975," I replied. After making a face that implied disbelief, he told me that he and pianist Mike Garson had already been touring together a few years before I was born. Before taking the job with Bowie, fresh from the record label fiasco, all my shows and day jobs and schooling, I had been feeling old at age 24. Suddenly, I was the baby of the band — which I found at times a challenging place to be, but also a gift. I thought I knew everything; but around all these folks, I knew I had to reevaluate that. This wondrous tour was a chance to absorb so much that I couldn't see in my solo career.

The TV shows we did in Europe were difficult. As a band, we loved to play, and often we would only be able to perform one song, which never felt satisfying. David would sometimes have to do interviews, and he could be delightfully snobby. He didn't suffer fools, and in his on-camera chats, he could talk anyone under the table. He could be cold, he could be warm. In almost every interview, he would inject the conversation with his poignant and fearless sense of humour, often launching into jokes that flew over most people's heads. And god forbid you call him a *chameleon* in 1999. He had heard it a million times before. My eyes started to roll when I heard that word, and I was convinced he was rolling his in his mind too.

David was also a lover of good experiences and great food. I remember when we were on tour in Denmark, someone had booked us into a restaurant, and our whole entourage strolled in, ready to have dinner together. When David got inside, he took one look around and said, "This is a fucking Pizza Hut!" He marched us out of there and took us all back to the hotel for some fine dining. He appeared to deeply admire his long-time right-hand woman, Coco, with whom he shared many secrets; he would often breathe a sigh of relief when she loved something new that the band was trying out. "Whew," he'd say a few times, if she dug one of his new ideas.

CLOSE TO HOME

David and I became close in an unexpected way when his son, Duncan, and I dated for a while. David was encouraging of this relationship in the beginning, but after some time together travelling and hanging out, it was clear to me that Duncan and I were on different paths. Our relationship only lasted about six months. In those early days, filmmaking was a seed in his young kid's heart, and I knew for certain he would become a filmmaker. I remember giving him a book about filmmaking and wrote something in the front about all the movies he would make. He did go on to realize those dreams, and in his work Duncan rose above what I know at times was a difficult role to play: the son of David Bowie.

Around the time we were together, I was renting an apartment in a house in New Paltz, New York, two hours north of Manhattan. I'd normally come in and out of the city by bus or car, and if Duncan was visiting from London, England, we'd spend some time hanging around New York or up at my tiny apartment near the Catskills. There were charming times between Duncan and me as boyfriend and girlfriend — visiting David's house in the Village, which I remember struck me more like a showroom than a lived-in home. And one day when Duncan and I lay in bed at my place, David phoned looking for Duncan, his voice in a more relaxed tone because he was in Dad mode, not Ziggy mode. "Do you have my watch?" he asked me before I passed the phone to Duncan. *Shit!* I said to myself. "Yes I do," I replied, remembering I had borrowed his astronomically expensive watch one day and accidentally taken it home after being in the studio. He wasn't mad. Little moments like this were a lovely glimpse at the normalcy of a legend. I guess sometimes everyone just wants to know, Hey, where's my stuff?

Bowie always wanted people around him to push themselves artistically, to find their musical groove, to do something of their own. At the same time, I can't deny that I loved glimpsing his life, the happy later-life days of someone who had given us iconic songs like "Moonage Daydream" and "Space Oddity," but now almost blended right into NYC life. After joining his band, I began to listen to his music more intently. I noticed complex rhythms and patterns that were cleverly disguised in the cloak of a pop song — things like the stealthily shifting synthesizer pattern in "Ashes to

Ashes." I lost myself inside the drawn-out quasi-prog rock of "Station to Station." Many people frown on covering songs as a way to grow, but I found from my time learning David's songs that this helped my own songwriting. The same can be true for anyone learning anyone else's music. **By learning other people's music, you are afforded the chance to get inside it, to see how harmonies are constructed and how musical parts fit together.**

David and I also shared a love of indie bands. I invited him out to see Grandaddy, a "space rock" outfit from Modesto that we both loved. The band couldn't believe David had come to see them, and I felt responsible for bringing everyone together, even if just for a few hours. David and I both loved recordings by Mercury Rev and Destroyer. Later, in the summer of 2015, we geeked out about our mutual adoration of Destroyer's "Times Square." Of course, if something sounded a little Bowie-esque but had a unique spirit of its own, David got right into it. Maybe it was because his influence stared back at him but had grown a little life of its own, a promise that as the years went on this would keep happening. New songs that contained a driving beat, '70s pianos, some rolling toms, big guitars, and glammed-up, daring vocals suggested this Bowie-inspired sound was immortal.

Being around David was both a history lesson and a party. The experiences I associate with him enriched my life in a way where the music, his words, his attitude, and his laughter seeped into my being, and instead of eclipsing the things I was still doing as a solo artist in Canada, the association with David super-charged me.

His humour was always intact. Like a little mouse popping in and out of a hole, it would emerge when you least expected it, sometimes dry wit, sometimes sarcasm. During rehearsals, I managed to find some time to write a song called "Asianblue" with with Mike Garson, an ambient piano and vocal ballad that clocked in under three minutes. Mike, David's long-time piano player, has an unmistakable-sounding style and has appeared on *Aladdin Sane*, *Young Americans*, *Diamond Dogs*, and several others. His style incorporates jazz and classical and relies heavily on improvisation. It was a thrill to write with Mike. One day, I played our quiet little number for David, eager to get his opinion. He listened, then he said to me, "Yeah, I like it, because it's short." He could be that way. He could give you the jabs like a big brother or a hug like a jovial father figure; but when he took to the stage, he exuded the star presence of both a supermodel and a man you might dream about forever. When he smiled at me onstage, I felt a flood of perfect happiness. He never gave a scowl or worried look if I made a mistake. If he'd put his arm around me or joke with me in front of the audience, it was warm and genuine, but also possessed a bit of comic relief. In those moments, I disappeared into the dream of rock 'n' roll. And then, because his flaws made him perfect, he would later get into the van back to the hotel, human like the rest of us, sometimes bitching about something that had irritated him. More than often, he'd just beam. Eventually, he'd be back to New York, finding his way like everybody else, savouring every moment of chaos and noise.

———

Cleaning up one Christmas, I found an old photograph that a fan had taken and sent to me. It was from the Serious Moonlight Tour. David looked like he was dressed in white linen and was on his tippy-toes doing some kind of crazy dance mid-song, hair bleached way too blond. I took a screenshot and sent it to David thinking he'd get a kick out of it. He wrote back the next day with an *LOL*. *Have a wonderful new year Emm.* He signed it: *dbx.* A week later, he was dead.

FOG

I found out David died when I got a text on January 11, 2016, from Holly with a string of broken hearts. It was six in the morning where I was, and I noticed there were vague messages of condolences in my Facebook inbox. I didn't know what they were for until I checked the news, and as in all of those earth-shifting moments that define us, my heart immediately weighed a thousand pounds and I broke down in tears. I was so confused because he had just put out *Blackstar*. We had just exchanged those emails. He was supposed to be here, to promote his new album in his enthusiastic, bubbly way, to talk to *Rolling Stone* and the *New York Times* . . . A fog lowered itself immediately into my life; all the feelings I had when I was on tour with him were unearthed, some I didn't know I had. At that time, in the formative years of my career, I wasn't aware of and hadn't formulated my *deeper* why. I had been searching for meaning, for more purpose; always on the hunt for love, some kind of embrace that would fill a void in me.

The opening chords of "Changes" and "Life on Mars?" were more than just famous sonic progressions, they had become soundtracks embedded deeply in my being — soundtracks to coming of age, to navigating the sweet and sour of life, to the miracle of being in the same room as this otherworldly teacher, singing songs that so many people adored. His songs had a life cycle: they grew from the 1960s, when he wrote as a young man wandering the world himself, to the experimental 1970s, the excessive 1980s, and into the 1990s, when he joyfully explored the ways technology, in both his music and his early forays into the internet, could be a vehicle for expression. What the world felt when he died, a collective teary sigh of a hero gone, felt different for me. I could not mourn him as a family member or even a close friend, yet I could not mourn him as a stranger. I dangled precariously between, as someone who shared the stage with him for a brief time and was influenced by him in ways far beyond musical style.

When David was gone, some friends around me cried like I did. Others told me to "get over it," to focus on my own family — that I had a job to do. But like a sapling turning into a tree that finally grows branches that hover and protect the world around it, my sadness over David's unexpected death and the mysterious album he left us cast a shadow. It was a shadow that sheltered me but pulled me down. This sadness could not be dealt with in a clean and easy way. Grief took its course and ruled my life for a time, despite the directives of those around me and the demands of life and children.

Over time, and only because of the gift of time, I experienced the fog of grief dissipate. As it lifted, something it may never do for those close to him, I began to think about the parts of him that brought joy: The curiosity for life, art, and music that lasted right up until his final days. The acceptance of his bandmates and others making music, whether they were from Hollywood or Forest, Ontario. The generosity that he would exude onstage, allowing everyone to have their moment, their name heard, and, sometimes, as happened to me in Europe one night, a moment of goofy interpretive dance to go along with one of his jokes.

Curiosity, acceptance, and giving. These are the lessons I learned from David Bowie — lessons I continue to take into my own life. Now, that decision I made in 1999, to veer from my path as a solo artist and go on the road with him, is one that I am so glad I made. The experience feels less of a detour and more an essential part of my story.

ACTION ITEMS

1. **Create space in your life to say yes to something that you're curious about.** Is there something you do that takes up so much of your time that it burns you out? Do you deal with an obligation that regularly drags you down? Is there a

responsibility that no longer fits into your life — to a person or a part of your job that no longer serves you? Let it go.

2. **Explore other people's music.** Cover songs, do karaoke, sing hymns — every successful artist I've ever known has had a curiosity for other people's music. Let it infuse you with wonder and inspire you instead of creating a sense of inferiority or competition.

3. **Listen and learn from others who have experienced more.** Don't assume that you know everything there is to know. "I know" can be one of the most dangerous starts to any phrase we have. Let go of feeling that you are the expert on all things, and see the beauty in opening up to new ideas and new thoughts.

4. **Video-record yourself performing.** I learned a lot by watching myself perform with David. Try this in your own work. You will learn so much about what kind of an artist and singer you are by being able to watch yourself perform. You will learn what works well and what doesn't, what translates and what distracts. Try different things in your performance — experiment with fashion, lighting, staging, as well as different microphones, amps, band set-ups, and sound systems. Everything you try will be an education, and one day you will find a way to present yourself and your music in its most energizing way.

CHAPTER 10

VOCAL HEALTH

"Successful people have good habits;
unsuccessful people have losery habits."
— JEN SINCERO

A year after I toured with Bowie, I was back on the road in Canada and one of my first big cross-country tours was approaching. I was worn out from all the touring I had been doing for the albums *Girl Versions* (2001) and *Asianblue* (2002). I was 27, jet-setting all around, and not particularly mindful of my voice. Despite the promise of the upcoming tour being a lucrative one, I found myself having vocal trouble. The tour, a co-headliner with a fellow Canadian rock 'n' roller named Holly McNarland, was all set. We had a tour bus, a string of dates in celebrated venues all across the country, and both Holly and I had stellar bands made up of energetic, experienced musicians. As more plans for the tour became solid, a deep discomfort settled in my gut. My voice really wasn't feeling right. I couldn't sing the way

I wanted. I feared that I might have to cancel my part in the tour.

It may amuse you to know that one of Toronto's foremost ear, nose, and throat doctors goes by the name of Dr. Hands. In his office waiting room are scores of framed eight-by-ten photos, hung all over the place, of actors and singers and stage stars whom he'd treated for various vocal maladies. I decided that the condition of my voice was bad enough to go to this celebrated doctor of vocal health.

As I sat in Dr. Hands's office, looking up at famous person after famous person immortalized in glossy black-and-white, I envisioned the doctor telling me I had vocal nodes, that I would need surgery, and I wouldn't be able to make music for at least a year. I started to think about plan B, whatever that was. Considering I was still riding the wave of being signed and singing with David, and I had fans who were eager to see me and buy my albums, this was going to be a serious blow.

An assistant called me into the examination room. I went in and sat down, fearful. Dr. Hands said a routine hello, asked some questions, and scoped my throat. He looked closely at my nasal cavity and vocal cords. This procedure, of him running a little camera down passageways in my nose and throat was nothing short of torture. I felt like I had been attacked from the inside by miniature aliens, and as the mini-aliens stopped slithering up against my eustachian tube orifice, I'd get the news that my career was kaput. After what felt like a decade, Dr. Hands finally pulled all of his apparatus from my passageways, pushed back on his swivel chair, and removed his latex gloves. "You're fine. Drink more water."

Stinging from the scope, but also confused by what he said, I scrunched up my eyebrows. "What?"

"You're dry. Drink one of these twice a day." He pointed to a one-litre bottle of water that was sitting on his desk and had a look on his face that said, *Now, out you go. I have a person more famous than you waiting to see me.* Out I skipped into the street, elated to not have to back out of the tour.

MORE SECRETS COURTESY OF
THE SPORTS WORLD

During my stint on CBC Radio many years later in 2018, the host I was shadowing that day asked me to come along to interview a local mixed martial arts champ for an upcoming segment. While at the studio, I struck up a conversation with one of the instructors, an older guy who looked like he knew everything about MMA. He talked to me about the sport and what kinds of things they do at the studio. In the course of our conversation, the instructor used a phrase that stuck with me. It was: "minimum effort, maximum power." The man used this phrase in reference to specific fighting moves that increase the chance of victory in the ring but conserve the energy of the athlete. It stuck with me. I thought "minimum effort, maximum power" could apply to a lot more in life. In fact, it could apply to everything.

Minimum effort, maximum power. That is how I see taking care of your voice. You don't need to do much to ensure your voice can thrive and be powerful.

Vocal health can lead you down a veritable rabbit hole. We've all heard how you shouldn't eat a brick of cheese before singing and that there are magical throat sprays and lozenges made from tree bark that can benefit your voice. Shelve all that for now and bear in mind **Secret No. 13: You're a singer all day long.** I say this because, once again, your instrument is on you. Because of singing's physical demands, you want to have a body that can heal itself easily and be strong.

Here are a few ways to optimize your vocal health all the time:

1. **Get more sleep.** Sleep makes everything better. Sleep is the athlete's steroid. Sleep is the singer's steroid. Sleep is one of our fundamental, base-level needs, and when we take it out of the equation, it's very hard to accomplish any other job or activity. If sleep is not something you're getting enough of, **explore habits around your pre-bedtime routine that may be making sleep difficult.** Common obstacles to sleep include stressful thoughts, phone use, alcohol consumption too close to bedtime, and exercise or caffeine too late in the day.

2. **Drink more water.** Hydration is so important! Water allows the vocal cords to retain their viscosity. When the vocal cords are dry, you lessen your chance of sounding full and rich. You tire more easily. Things sound rough and feelings are harder to express. This is the single most important healthy step you can take to ensure a top-notch voice. Take it from me — your audience will thank you. I've heard singers onstage when they are dry and tired from touring and it tires *me* out to listen

to them. Water also, as we know, flushes out the body, and when we keep hydrated we are simply healthier overall. So, **put hydration on your list of priorities**. Many people just don't think about it. They don't enjoy drinking water, they are too busy to stop and hydrate, they neglect foods that are rich in water like cucumbers, celery, and watermelon. A while ago I committed to starting every day with a glass of room temperature water. I put it by my bed the night before and because it's there when I wake up in the morning, I am more apt to down it. I have my water before coffee, and this habit makes a massive difference in my life. If you start with coffee, you're starting from a place of dehydration. You've already been sleeping for hours without hydrating, so opt for the water first.

3. **Humidify.** Make sure your living environment, particularly where you sleep, is not too dry. Ideally, you want the humidity in the room to be between 30 and 50 percent. Any less than 30 percent, and you'll notice your skin can get dry. Fingers, feet, and lips can crack in a cold climate, and your voice can feel thin and dry. Balance is important, however. Any more than 50 percent humidity and exotic plants will begin to grow out of your floorboards. **Get a humidity meter and test the humidity level in your living and sleeping environments.** How could you improve on this? Take action in the form of getting a humidifier, lowering the heat in the house or that room, boiling water in a pot on the

stove (just don't burn your house down), or putting a humidifier on your furnace.

4. **Don't make yelling a regular habit.** Yelling stresses the vocal flaps; it irritates them and lessens their ability to work well. Not to mention, humans look really ugly when they yell. Unless you are saving a baby from crossing the I-95, there's no need to yell. Sometimes we need to scream, shout, and yell the F-word, and that's all well and good, but if you are a consistent yeller, see if you can find a way to channel that energy into something else. We need to feel and express rage and anger — especially as women who have not traditionally been encouraged to do so. But for a long time, I was channeling those emotions into yelling. This was not the best way to honour my anger. If you find yourself consistently taking things out on people (like I did for a long time), ask yourself what the underlying cause might be. We can explore our feelings through friendship, therapy, looking at childhood triggers, being honest with ourselves about what we truly need in life or what we would like to see happen. Sounds like a lot of trudging through a landmine of difficult emotions, but this is where change happens. Recognizing triggers as places where you need to do a little soul work — this is where you can come out the other side, possessing awareness and feeling more in touch with your authentic self.

5. **Don't smoke or vape.** Obvious. *But David Bowie smoked*, you might say. *Joni Mitchell smoked! Aretha*

Franklin smoked! All the great singers of our time smoked! While this is true, some singers grew up in a time where cigarettes were considered nerve-calming and healthy. Today, enough research exists and enough humans have died from lung-related illnesses due to smoking that we all know we shouldn't smoke. You can also inspect for yourself and hear how each of the above singers' voice changed over time, and sometimes not for the better. Smoking can lead to loss of range and control as well as to serious breathing difficulties.

After my break-up, I became a smoker. I saw a cigarette as a reward for trudging through life's barbed wires. A brief moment outside on the step, away from the house and chores, taking in the sunshine and feeling like a '70s rock star for a minute. I understand what it's like to not want to give up something like this. Only after really believing that it wasn't good for me was I able to shift course.

Sometimes it helps to answer these kinds of questions: Do you *want* to give it up? What would your life look like if you gave up a nagging bad habit? Who around you enables or encourages this habit? In what ways can you move towards changing a habit that you don't like? If you don't give it up, are you willing to live with the consequences? Consider all the options so that you can look at your behaviours clearly. For more serious issues, reach out to a professional who specializes in addiction. Addiction often has very real underlying triggers and sometimes everyday remedies are simply not enough. If you want to make a serious change on a serious issue, you have to attack it with, yup, you guessed it, a crapload of seriousness. There's no shame in admitting that you need help. If all of us admitted that we needed help sometimes, our world would be way, way, way better off.

6. **Cardio.** Nothing will activate your lungs better than doing some regular cardio. The more the better, but at minimum try for three sessions per week where you're pushing yourself for at least 20 minutes. I ran a half-marathon a few years ago, and my voice was never better than it was then.

———

That's all — six things to start you on your way. These are bare minimum habits that the majority of top-level singers live by as well.

ACTION ITEMS

1. **Pick one habit from the above list and work towards it.**

CHAPTER 11

HELLO YOU, MEET YOU

"As long as you love who you are — your morals,
your values, that type of stuff — you're okay."
— NICKI MINAJ

After touring with Bowie ended, I continued to record with
him. We went into Sear Sound and Looking Glass Studios
in New York to record an album called *Toy*, which featured
renditions of songs he wrote in the 1960s. By this time, the
Bowie band — its old and new members — found ourselves
bonded by history, travel, music itself, and our recent big,
successful concerts. David and I would continue to have
conversations about fashion and music, and we even once
during recording fell asleep on a couch together like a couple of lazy house cats. I called him Daddy Stardust and
he called me Egg, a nickname given to me by Mark Plati,
derived from my initials. Although I was living the pinnacle
of hired gun life and napping with legends, I was itching to

return to Canada where I could get back to my own indie pop career, writing songs and making my own records.

I returned to Toronto, where I had been voted Favourite Female Musician the previous year in a poll put out by Toronto's *Eye Weekly* magazine. The phone was ringing a lot. Although I returned with a fierce curiosity to make more of my own music, I quickly learned that everybody wanted to talk about my time with Bowie. At the risk of sounding spoiled, this felt conflicting to me. Bowie and my time with him was all anyone wanted to talk about, yet there was no clear answer as to whether I might be invited back to tour with him. And if I got invited back, would I go? In interviews with journalists, the questions about my own work always came after questions like, "What is he like?"

Eventually, David hired Catherine Russell, who covered both my and Holly's roles in the band. What a powerhouse she was. If I was disappointed by David hiring Catherine, I buried it and moved on.

———

Thrust out in the world, energized but lost, I did what anyone does at that moment — I packed bags and travelled. I went back to a place that had always been a haven for me — England — and there, amidst the commotion of London and the rolling hills of the Cotswolds, I explored, let myself breathe, and took time for me. I played piano in the quaint music rooms you could rent by the hour at Belsize Park. I met up with musician friends like Bernard Butler and Mikey

Rowe who played keys with Oasis, I went out to clubs in Camden and Soho, and I went to all the art galleries. I later wandered off solo into neighbouring places. I lay on the beaches of Brittany. I saw the south of France. I dreamed up plans for new original music. I went to concerts. One of them was back in England at Reading Festival, where I experienced a thrilling set by Beck, in which he plowed through all of his trippy indie hits, part punk and part pop, and then at the tail end of his encore, he and the band threw down their instruments and covered the entire stage in caution tape as the crowd cheered. The audience was left, music buzzing in our ears, to witness a "crime scene" littered with feedback frequencies and Year 2000 indie-punk abandon. Where were we all headed? As a society? As a world? We didn't know. And when it came to my own life, I didn't have a clue either.

Inspired by meeting Joe Elliott from Def Leppard after the Dublin show with Bowie, I created a piano ballad version of "Pour Some Sugar on Me," which I sent to Joe as a Christmas present. Joe loved it and this song spawned the album *Girl Versions*, which saw me take songs sung by men and transform them with my voice. I took Ozzy's "Crazy Train" and slowed it down to a sentimental piano and vocal ballad. People who had been listening to that song for years finally heard the words clearly. In a version of "Waiting Room" by Fugazi, I did the same but added cello. Songs by Blur, Nick Cave, Death Cab for Cutie, and Robert Wyatt also appeared on the record. *Girl Versions* twisted the lyrics of men and turned the meanings of songs on their heads because suddenly everything was in a female voice. These cover versions were everything from absurd to poignant in their new forms. The album was nominated for Pop Album of the Year at the Juno Awards. I didn't win, but in true Emm fashion, tenacious and curious, I enjoyed the glow of the nod and moved on.

It's hard to know yourself completely at age 25 or 26, unless you possess some astute awareness or a high level of objectivity. I can say unequivocally that I did not possess either of these and, during these years, acted more like a sponge. After coming off the road with David, I tried to write songs like him. I read books he thought I should read (about Mod fashion). I even tried to emulate what I saw in my travels — like covering the stage with caution tape at the end of one of my own shows after witnessing Beck's set-closing antics. There was no harm in testing these things out, but they often fell flat. I was trying things on, but I was also beginning to lose sight of my true self.

LOS ANGELES

After our working relationship started to sour, I stopped working with Michael Murphy, moved to LA, and hired Allison, my former A&R woman from the Mercury days, to be my manager. Allison was brazen and outspoken, Hollywood through and through. She was connected and had a new job at Hollywood Records. Daunted but inspired by my time with David, I probably saw Allison as possessing some of the ballsy traits that I lacked at the time. "Emm, you're wearing *lipstick*!" she'd exclaim as we hit the dog-piss-scented trail at Runyon Canyon, yelling it with so much horror, you'd think I had a second head growing out of my shoulder and didn't know it.

Yes, I was settling into a new life in LA. I had made a splash with *Science Fair* and now with *Girl Versions*, but in my new role as a sponge, my spine was getting more malleable by the day. Under the Hollywood sun, I started to drift back to the idea of signing a major record deal. Deep inside, I knew signing again would demand things of me that were not right for me. I might have been dumped off Mercury and thrust unexpectedly into a world of indie rock, but that world of do-it-yourself was a good place for me to be. My record label motto was "DIY or die." I even had little badges made with the slogan on it, and fans had begun to repeat the phrase on their blogs and in online forums. I required space, creativity, control, freedom, and the phone ringing just a little less. But, like an artist who had not defined a clear path for herself, I allowed myself to be tempted by the allure of having more. I could be selling more records, I told myself.

Named after the three-minute song I wrote with Mike Garson, I started work on *Asianblue*, my next album, with producer Wally Gagel, who had made some pretty poptastic records with bands like Folk Implosion and Eels. Every day, I'd truck off to his studio in trendy Silver Lake, writing as I drove. We were crafting big pop songs that sounded nothing like my usual work. In a rationale that exemplified how out of touch I was with myself, I figured, "sounding like me" had only yielded moderate success; I needed to sound a little "not like me" to compete with the Janet Jacksons of the world. Wally and I wrote some bona fide pop hits with big beats and big choruses. Even on September 11,

2001, when I was awoken by my boyfriend, Sean, telling me that commercial planes had been flown into the World Trade Center, I took it in, heard him say "this means war," compartmentalized it, then shoved my stuff in my purse and went to work with Wally. To this day, my song "Young Rebel," with its trippy beats and minor-key tonality, will always remind me of that day — a day I just went to work, pretending nothing had happened. That day, I just kept singing. Turning a blind eye to one of the most catastrophic days of our generation shows how delusion had become part of my daily routine.

Through the making of this album, Allison guided me like a straight-shooting businesswoman and a catty sister. After our morning strolls up Runyon Canyon, we'd get coffee at the Coffee Bean and Tea Leaf and riff about the music industry. We'd dissect people's singles, tear apart the personalities of old male music industry heads, and I'd get the lowdown on who was going batshit crazy behind the scenes. She gave me a mountain of advice and, with it, a boatload of complaints about her own life: work, her dogs, her past. The complaints were peppered by wisdom and heart, and if I'd had more clarity back then, I would have known that underneath the barbed words, the emotional baggage, the near–traffic accidents, and misguided criticism, beat a heart of gold.

One of the things Allison believed was that we could approach Capitol Records with the songs I was recording with Wally. Desperate to prove that I could eclipse my time with Bowie and get some journalists asking about *me* for once, I went all in. I worried that I wasn't really an indie queen like the Toronto papers said. Maybe I was just a failed major label artist who could — possibly — rise again. After my songs made the rounds to the usual music execs, I zipped up my olive-green Juicy Couture velvet hoodie, glued on the fake eyelashes that I had learned to apply during the Bowie tour, and Allison and I went in for a meeting in the iconic Capitol Records building, a structure that had been designed to look like a stack of records, one hit piled on top of another.

On the day of our meeting, I walked in and sat across the room from Andrew Slater. A former music critic who had been brought into Capitol to transform the place, he was supposed to be a bit of a rebel and a big deal. Looking more like a musician than a record exec, Andy's claims to fame included producing Fiona Apple's *Tidal* and working with the Wallflowers. Andy played fancy guitars, and they were strewn around the room. His office was as big as a living room, with a sitting area off to one corner and his desk the size of a dining table at the other end. The view, astounding. But the minute I walked in, it felt like the spotlight was not really on me, it was on Andy. With every word I said, and there weren't many, I faded deeper and deeper into the background. Why did I wear this stupid hoodie? Should I have bedazzled it? was all I could think, knowing somewhere deep inside that I was losing.

"I'll never tell you why Andy didn't want to sign you," said Allison a week or so later, during one of our walks up the canyon. I felt those words sting for a few years after she said them. The laceration of never knowing, of feeling not worthy enough to demand the answer.

MONTREAL

Not long after, fueled by the events of 9/11 and wanting to be closer to family, I came back to Canada. As I crossed the border, the news shifted from Osama bin Laden and the attack on America to a CBC feature on the best way to take care of houseplants. Billboards along the freeway advertising everything from lawyers to Applebee's restaurants were replaced by tall swaying trees. The constant glow of the sun was gone. The lens had changed. Just as I began to recognize the devastating impact of 9/11, I lay to rest that straggling desire to sign a record deal. I thought about the families who lost their loved ones, the smoke that had so seriously affected firefighters and residents in New York. I thought about the terror of man's unkindness, and the ways in which we as a society couldn't see or comprehend each other's views on religion and politics. Now it had to come to this. What really mattered — family, home, stability, and certainty — began to come into view for me.

My boyfriend and I moved our life into a brownstone in Montreal belonging to folk singer Kate McGarrigle. I loved being around Kate — she was a strong woman who loved music and loved her life in Montreal. She and her sister Anna would rehearse in the apartment above us, their beautiful harmonies and French lyrics wafting down through the floorboards. As for me and my boyfriend, our future was uncertain, my sense of self was slipping further and further out of view, and soon I had said yes to getting married.

What the hell does any of this have to do with your singing career? A lot.

Knowing who you are, what works for you as an artist and singer, and what kind of life you want to lead is going to help you — in work, in play, in everything. When life muddies up your sense of self, or you possess a narrow or skewed sense of yourself, decision-making becomes very difficult. And when you make poor decisions, you usually end up living with the consequences: We are held back from achieving what we want. Obstacles slow us down, sometimes for years.

Then, there is the actual mystery of not knowing who you are as a performer. Why does standing still onstage looking like a supermodel, hardly moving around, work wonders for Swedish chanteuse Nina Persson but not for Mick Jagger? Why does wrapping your stage in caution tape work for Beck and not for a Canadian singer-songwriter? Why do ten-inch heels make sense for Gaga but might not for Sarah McLachlan? Why is being on a label perfect for one artist and a creative disaster for another? Why can some people sing country music so well while others sound less authentic doing it? Why are some people suited to singing soft indie rock hits and others to belting out stuff? Why would Queen Latifah doing an album of yodelling be confusing to people? Or maybe it wouldn't.

The landscape of making music and functioning within it can seem so confusing. It took me many, many years to get to the bottom of what works for me as a person, an artist, a singer, and a performer. Here is the part of the book where I save you about two decades of self-exploration and soul-searching by offering some tips on getting a little closer to both finding your authentic self and knowing what kind of a performer you're meant to be.

EGO

The definition of the ego varies depending where you look. One source says that it means "self-esteem," but the Cambridge Dictionary definition as it relates to psychoanalysis, describes ego as **"the part of a person's mind that tries to match the hidden desires (= wishes) of the id (= part of the unconscious mind) with the demands of the real world."**

Deepak Chopra, always a decent alternative to the dictionary, says, "The Ego is not who you really are. The ego is your self-image; it is your social mask; it is the role you are playing. Your social mask thrives on approval. It wants control, and it is sustained by power, because it lives in fear."

One thing is for sure, there's a load of literature and opinion on ego, and to really understand and dissect it would require another set of books. Despite our understanding of its presence in our lives, and the general feeling that operating from it can result in unfulfillment and discontent, we still move through life allowing ego to be a major influence. Musicians and entertainers are especially susceptible to the pitfalls of ego because our very work involves inviting in the outside world. We tell ourselves that we can't get video views if someone doesn't want to look at us. We won't get followers if people don't love everything we say and sing about. We won't even have an audience if we aren't something interesting to look at — either as sexy as a runway model or as moody as a singer in a death-metal band. Pleasing people is often the root of what we are doing, so why on earth would we try to get rid of the ego? Is it even possible if we wanted to?

Marta Brzosko is a writer and blogger. Splashed across the header of her Self-Awareness Blog is the declaration: "Sick and tired of self-improvement. Advocating for self-awareness instead." In her post, "Ego Death: Why Trying to Kill the Ego Won't Work for Spiritual Seekers," Marta writes a long and poignant essay about making the choice to befriend your ego.

"Trying to get rid of your ego carries all kinds of traps," she wrote in May 2020. "Enhanced self-hatred, spiritual bypass or getting addicted to the 'spiritual high' while discarding the seemingly mundane, everyday experience — these are just some examples. Maybe the experience of ego death is worth risking them.

"[…] there's a gentler and more compassionate approach. You have a choice.

"If you decide to make friends with your ego, you can treat each step on your path as valid. Even when the ego screams for attention, you can remember that this is just a part of being human."

Another trap of trying to decode the ego's role in your life is a reluctance to be open to all the possibilities on the path to happiness as a creator and human. Seeing things as "all or nothing" or "black and white" is common. We're either famous or we're not. We're successful or we're not. We're great or we suck. This way of viewing life is suffocating. "All or nothing thinking" is one of the cognitive distortions laid out in Cognitive Behavioural Therapy, a type of short-term therapy that involves changing thought patterns. In reality, life is never really cut and dry — our experiences are made up of a patchwork of influences and emotions, and what we decide in life, how we decide it, and what we plan for can have a wide, malleable variety of outcomes.

Instead of beating myself up for the negative effects of ego, I've found more success in a gentle exploration of how the external might be affecting my internal world. Once I see what isn't helping me shine, clues to finding authentic joy become easier to recognize. I didn't even know what the ego was for most of my life, yet it was guiding me and my music in the most severe way.

Eckhart Tolle's writing can be a great gateway to understanding ego. *The Power of Now* and *A New Earth: Awakening to Your Life's Purpose* are two of his books that are worthwhile companions when it comes to looking at ego and living from a place of consciousness. Once you can wrap your head around the science of the mind and its response to what's happening around us, you can separate emotion from reason and make decisions about your career more clearly. I mean, what's the point of having millions of fans if you're not a fan of yourself? Checking the ego can lead to becoming very clear on personal and professional values. Outcome: Happiness. Acceptance. Clarity.

VALUES

Values are the things in life that we have decided are important. They can form our highest vision of ourselves. Integrity is what we feel when we uphold our values. Our values can be things like honesty, self-respect, respect for others, loyalty, and commitment. It's important to know what your values are because they create a framework for what you will do in your life and how you will do it. For example, if honesty is one of your values, you would not tolerate cheating on a spouse or stealing from a friend. If self-respect is one of your values, you would not harm yourself or neglect your own self-care.

Problems come when we are not clear on our values. With very few of us moving through life without emotional baggage or triggers, it means that we can easily veer away from our vision of integrity by responding to baggage and emotional triggers in ways that compromise our values. This might sound like it has nothing to do with singing, but it is actually very important. Because I wasn't clear on my own values, I allowed myself to waste so many years wondering about what was right for me as an artist. In a lot of cases, I'd go with what the last person said to me. This was easy to do because I was young, eager, and not clear on what I would tolerate and not tolerate. Boundaries help us uphold our values, and if we lack self-respect, we feel guilty for setting boundaries. If this sounds like we could all use ongoing psychotherapy and lots of it, it's probably true. But this simple concept of knowing your values can help your life in immeasurable ways. One thing to examine as you try to stay true to your values and check your ego is, yup, the thing that, for some of us, adults "ruined": our childhood.

CHILDHOOD STUFF

The whole time we are young our minds are being mapped. Our brains are literally growing and forming new neural pathways. During childhood and adolescence, we absorb information consciously and subconsciously, and that means we take in the good, the bad, and everything in between in a way that stamps us for life. Sound scary? Damn right it is. When I became a parent, I became very uneasy with this sense of having so much influence over another human. Just as easily as I could train my two-year-old daughter to sing "Changes" by Bowie and "Big Yellow Taxi" by Joni Mitchell, I would also be showing her a glimpse of how a woman lives, responds to life, and deals with everything from frustration to frivolity.

When we find ourselves having issues later in life, in relationships, career, health, mindset, and so on, quite often the root of our difficulties is a result of the attitudes, events, and behaviours that were burned into our psyche as children. We watched our parents act and react around issues of love, money, sex, religion, and politics, and the behaviours they modelled for us would shape us forever. Whether we liked it or not, and even if they were just trying their best, we were the pawns in Oceania and they were the Ministry of Truth, to reference Orwell's *1984*.

But this is where integrity can swoop in like a superhero. If we know our values, we can live in alignment with them. If we are unclear on our values, that's when baggage from childhood can come to kick shit in. Our energy around doing good and living well becomes drained. If living a life of harmony is important to you, but all you remember are parents who slammed doors and threw planters at each other, you may come up against problems in your own relationships with believing that harmony can be achieved at all. If you were told as a child that you were a crappy singer, you move through life thinking that you are, indeed, a crappy singer. What's worse is that because these attitudes were planted when we were too young to reject them, we go through life thinking that we are worthless and at fault.

NEEDS

Needs are part of being human. We all have them, yet we don't always acknowledge how important they are to us. I moved through most of my life "going by feel" as it pertained to my needs. As a businessperson and an artist, this was a drain on my energy and resources. Only recently, as I established my values and looked at my childhood baggage, did I admit that I have very specific needs. By the time I was in my 40s, I realized some of these needs, such as love and connection, had not been met for ages. I also noted that most of my needs were simply impossible to meet if very basic needs were not met first, such as sleep. Hands up any parents suffering from lack of sleep? I see you.

In 2018, during a tour of the US, I broke up one of my long drives by staying at a fellow songwriter's house in Syracuse. Bea Talplacido was a thriving singer-songwriter, a single mom with a handsome boyfriend from Brooklyn, and possessed of a lovely energy of resilience and badassery. She opened her home to me to stay the night. In the morning, over breakfast, I asked her how she did it all. We talked about books that inspired her and then she talked about needs. She told me that when she feels low, she examines a set of needs that she knows have to be met in order to live a full, whole life. I left her house thinking about her very simple answer, and also how I had simply not made that list of needs for myself. But then more occurred to me: I hadn't quite looked at or bothered to understand what behaviours I regularly exhibited — aka my personality.

From Maslow's hierarchy of needs to Gretchen Rubin's book *The Four Tendencies*, I dove headlong into the subject of human behaviour and needs. There are countless ways to investigate and measure aspects of your personality. The Myers-Briggs test offers a look at your personality type through a series of questions and evaluations. The Enneagram test is a dive into the human psyche that numbers your personality and gives a detailed reading for each number that explains why we are motivated to do different things. Astrology and human design both have a similar appeal to humans as a means of explaining why we act the way we do.

Science, and whether or not it agrees with these modalities, is no match for your instincts. The approach that opened my eyes was reading Gretchen Rubin's *The Four Tendencies: The Indispensable Personality Profiles that Reveal How to Make Your Life Better (and Other People's Lives Better, Too)*. In it, Rubin breaks all of humanity into four personality types and goes into great detail about how people with these personalities can live in a way that maximizes their potential. She even writes about how to coexist with other personality types and how to optimize your circumstances with the knowledge of who you are. Sound way too simple and totally nuts? It could be, but Rubin's book was a gateway to really looking at myself. After reading her book, I identified as an *obliger*. This explained years and years of people-pleasing and feeling inadequate, a role I stepped into with ease when I became a mother. I put everyone before myself, thinking that was what a mother does. Anyone reading this who is a parent knows that the over-used analogy of "putting your oxygen mask on before putting it on someone else" is actually hella true. I noticed that much of my unhappiness stemmed from 1) not being clear on my values (which led to confusion over what I would tolerate and not tolerate), and 2) living life as this obliger and neglecting myself.

Now that I know that I'm an obliger, I can recognize when I am about to give too much to others in a way that's going to end up in a huge messy explosion of resentment and self-neglect. Now, I accept that I like to help and please others, but I create boundaries so that I honour *my* needs. By honouring my needs, I can actually be helpful to others in the right way.

One of the joys of getting older is that through experience, trial and error, defining our values, and learning from others, we can start to see our needs more clearly. If I look back to that meeting at Capitol Records in Los Angeles, equipped with some of the a-ha moments I have just listed, I would have seen that I needed to be heard by Andy Slater

— not just in regard to my music, but in that office that day. I would have made sure my voice was heard. Or at very least, I would have been able to see that the way the meeting had gone was a clue that Andy Slater and Capitol Records was not a good fit for *me*. If I had been aware of my childhood triggers, I might have been able to recognize that my needs as an individual needed to be acknowledged just as much as my needs as an artist.

Seeing our needs clearly can be liberating. Once I was able to eventually face the truth that some of my very specific needs needed to be met, life and living as an artist became far less exhausting. Without the basic need of sleep being met and sometimes good nutrition (two things that all too frequently go by the wayside in the early days of parenting), I realized none of my other needs could even be looked at. Without acknowledging my need for a certain level of financial income and making it a reality, I couldn't give properly to others on an album or a concert. Without deep commitment and a healthy love relationship, I had trouble actualizing my highest self.

The day that I admitted that I have needs, a crap load of them, some of them basic and some of them formidable, I could better uphold my values. With integrity intact, life's puzzle pieces, once scattered all over the table of my mind and heart, easily fell into place. And with the puzzle pieces connected, I could do the work to move towards creative growth and success without being drained, constantly confused why life wasn't working in my favour. **Secret No. 14: Know your values and know what you need.**

ACTION ITEMS

1. **What are your values? What do you stand for? Write them down.** Be clear on them. If this is tough to do, ask yourself, Who do I want to be at my highest level? What are the values that the best version of myself would hold dear and will not tolerate being compromised?

2. **What formative events from the past are you ready to stop hanging onto?** This is a hugely important and sometimes heavy action item and may require therapy or other support. Cognitive Behavioral Therapy (CBT) is a good treatment if you are looking to change thought patterns and beliefs that have been holding you back. Many therapists are trained in CBT, and there are several workbooks that centre around CBT if you decide to explore this further.

3. **Admit that you have needs.** Whether you use a behavioural identification model, read a book, engage in therapy, or just set up a tent in the backyard and don't come in the house for 11 days, know what you need. **Write down what is important to you and what needs you absolutely must have met in order to shine.**

4. **Hire a performance coach or a mentor.** Performance coaches can really help curate your stage show and provide objectivity on what works and what doesn't. Sometimes a musical director can help with this, too, but a performance coach (sometimes

they double as vocal coaches) typically can give feedback that goes beyond the music. They can advise on movement, stage set-up, dancing, and overall presence. If you think someone in your life with some knowledge on this could serve as your performance coach or mentor, invite them into your world — as long as you trust their judgment and feel safe enough to receive their feedback.

Part 3

WORKING IT AND MAKING IT WORK

CHAPTER 12

SOUND AND BODY

"Lightning makes no sound until it strikes."
— MARTIN LUTHER KING JR.

SO A FAN WANTS TO KILL YOU;
WHAT IS THE TAKEAWAY?

One day, around the year 2000, I received an order of ten Emm Gryner T-shirts from a guy named Ron from New York state. Ten T-shirts! All the same design. This is great, I thought. Ron must be running a baseball team of people who love piano-based pop music about heartbreak. I pocketed the few hundred dollars and sent out the shirts. Then Ron wrote again. And again. Then he sent emails. By the time all was said and done, I received about three hundred letters and emails from Ron, whose expressions of deep adoration for me and my music eventually evolved into sexually abusive language and death threats. Ron wrote that he had been to my home. He talked about slitting my throat, torturing me, killing me, and the tipping point was when he began to mention the names of people I loved and his intentions to hurt them. He also threatened to blow up the offices at the Time Warner building in New York, something my team and I took seriously and contacted police about, as well as the Time Warner offices, who did not respond.

He also posed as other people, and talked about himself, writing he had been "alarmed by Ron's messages which detailed a murder/suicide mission." All of Ron's letters were typed in a combo of CAPS!, strange s p a c i n g and lower case characters, all wrapped up in **--peculiar--**, non/ SENSICAL! punctuation. I was appalled and shaken to my core.

Having an abusive fan like this was something of an anomaly for me. By the time Ron had targeted me, I was an independent artist with a relatively small fan base. I had always encountered people who were jazzed about my music, and expressed as much, but this scenario was different. I felt threatened and unsafe, confused about what to do next. Eventually, it occurred to me that Ron could have a mental health issue, so I would have to handle everything in a different way than if it were an everyday conflict.

I approached a colleague of mine at the time, Joni Daniels, a beautiful red-haired lady from Toronto who had worked with me for many years as an administrator and manager. Joni, who shared my birthday of June 8, was a kindred spirit and also knew the ins and outs of the music business, having worked for years as a producer for MuchMusic.

I spun around in a swivel chair at her Toronto office, which was in a penthouse overlooking Lake Ontario. "What do I do about this?" I asked Joni. We had already had some conversations with police, reaching out in both New York and Toronto.

"Well, you could go to the police again," I remember her saying. "But by getting a restraining order, you open up a dialogue with that person."

What Joni was suggesting, with which I agreed, was that suddenly there would "be something" between this person and me. Even though it would be a court document meant to keep me safe, it would still be something tying me to Ron.

The more I thought about it, the more I disliked the idea of getting a restraining order. I wanted to control my reaction to the problem, not become further entrenched in the situation. It's a thought process so many survivors struggle with — whether to come forward or deal with it privately in one's own way. I chose the latter. It was what was right for me at the time.

Police, in previous talks, had indicated that cutting off all contact with Ron was advisable. I was to simply state that his correspondence was unwelcome and then never engage again. I did this, but when I got back to my home in LA, I felt like doing more. I decided I would help put this whole thing behind me and take some control by researching self-defence classes. Ahh yes, the self-defence class. One mention and it can conjure up images of pastel-clad women with minimal upper-body strength, learning to knee men in the balls and run away, our handbags full of makeup flapping behind us. But the self-defence class can also be seen as just one more thing in our lives to accept and endure as humans born with ovaries.

The class I chose was an eight-week course held near Universal Studios in the Valley, about 20 minutes from my home in West Hollywood. I signed up alone, as most of my close girlfriends were back in Toronto. Buddies at my side or not, I was going to do what I needed to do. I was going to learn to fight back.

I arrived at my first class feeling like it was the first day of high school. There I was, all of five-foot-two, with towering girls all around, probably 25 in total. I'd later learn some of these women were supermodels Kirsty Hume and Guinevere van Seenus, who had walked runways all over the world. The fact that some of us held office jobs and others of us had been on the cover of *Vogue* eventually melted into one big pile of "who cares?" Before long, all of us in this class were feeling the commonality of being survivors and seekers. We focused intently on the tasks at hand, looking to transform past painful moments in our lives with knowledge and preparedness. My heart sank a little when a group of women rallied lovingly around one person in the class, who clearly had been through something deeply painful. Whatever it was that had brought her there was fresh and raw. The tears were visible and her pain was palpable.

The program we were in, called Impact Self-Defense, required us to engage in full-contact fighting with men in protective suits. In what was maybe the most difficult exercise we had to do, we would fight our way out of mock rape scenarios. This was an exercise dreaded by each of us, whether it triggered actual memories or was something utterly foreign. This was no "knee a guy in the balls" course, it was a "throw yourself to the wolves" trial by fire.

THE GIFT OF SOUND

During my class, the instructor would teach us how to quickly form a "relationship" with an assailant that would allow us to get out of an assault in the most optimal way. We also learned to strike an attacker in the heat of the moment (putting fingernails into eyeballs or crushing the vulnerable bones of the foot with heels). We learned the immense power of the lower body and how to derive power from this area (sound familiar?), even when on the ground. I quickly noticed how incredibly more effective I was in my attack movements when I yelled "No!" with every hit. Now, even though I loved to sing and was comfortable with making noise by this point, I sure didn't feel very cool — a short, shy woman yelling "NO!" while stabbing a guy in what looked like a fat suit with her short, boyish nails. At some point, I longed for the quiet life of childhood and chickens, those treasured quiet years when *feeling the heat* meant that your Hypercolor shirt would betray you when you gazed too lovingly at Larry Wilcox from *CHiPs* on the TV screen. But life was different now, and like a lot of girls in the room, I was desperate to find compassion and justice given the imbalance and inequalities I saw in society. I needed to know how to deal with a life and death situation, even if I hated that these situations even existed. I sucked it up, and

I told myself the story that this was the price of selling and performing my music in the modern age. If the world wasn't going to change anytime soon, then I would.

Yelling "no" every time I fought back surprised me and super-charged me. My power became immense. Yelling "no" from my gut helped maximize my physical power, focus my return attack, and deliver way more force. The mind-blowing power of "No!" was my first glimpse into the incredible transformative energy of making sound. Yes, in a previous chapter I advised you not to yell as a way to maintain your vocal health — but this is different.

The day after my Impact graduation, which was an emotionally and physically draining day, I could barely move as a result of being bruised from all the activities; despite this, I was already considering going on to more advanced classes, some of which involved learning how to protect myself against multiple assailants carrying weapons. Even though I still haven't taken more classes, I'll always remember the feelings of satisfaction and empowerment with what I had learned from just one course. When all was said and done, self-defence training opened my heart and mind to the benefits of channeling anger into fighting for good, my own good, for and with other women. The class, and how I used my voice, was a step towards recalling my own self-worth and my own power when it had been slipping through my hands as a result of the dance with ego and the music business.

Ironically, the letters and correspondence from Ron died down after I completed the course. I heard from some other female artists that he had sent them similar letters. I was relieved to be free of his intrusion into my life.

———

A few years later, sure that he had lost interest in me, I was caught off-guard when Ron showed up out of the blue at my concert at a popular songwriter's venue called The Point in Bryn Mawr, Pennsylvania. Sporting mirrored wrap-around sunglasses, he sat alone, cold and still. He positioned himself three rows from the stage, just close enough to be unnerving. When I first spotted him, I was alarmed. All of his threats flooded back to me, and I milled around in the tiny dressing room short of breath. I envisioned having to interact with him after the show. I envisioned having to walk my gear out to my car alone and wondered if he'd be waiting in the dark. But as my set time neared, I shelved those thoughts. Other fans were eager to hear me, some had travelled from neighbouring states, and I owed it to them to put on a good show. I took to the stage and I recalled my Impact training, the moves I made, the sounds, the feels, the bruises, the tears, and the other women around me. I thought about how it was in that class that I took things into my own hands and that if I did it then, I could do the same onstage. I started to sing.

I sang and sang better than I had in a long time. I surprised myself. I was able to sing every song and look Ron dead in the eyes, past the sunglasses, past the chilling demeanor, and I felt fear dissipate. Every lyric came out with the tenderness and angst with which it was written. With every note, I seemed to rise up, buzzed from a self-assured concoction of progress and forgiveness.

Where I once yelled no, I now sang my own words and slowly dismantled any feelings of intimidation or fear.

I never heard from Ron or saw him again.

Secret No. 15: Your power is in you.

THE HISTORY OF SINGING

Sound: a truly miraculous thing. That we have the power to make it is just amazing. That making sound originated as an innate need just might be at the root of our passion for singing.

"Men sang out their feelings long before they were able to speak their thoughts," writes Otto Jespersen in his book *Language: Its Nature, Origin and Development*. Jespersen writes that the first sounds of humans were exclamations, not efforts to communicate. The noises we made were like the singing of birds and the roaring of animals. The sounds we made were like the "crooning of babies" and they came from a gut desire and an inner craving. The sounds we made as humans in early days didn't exist to entertain, appease, or express to other creatures. Jespersen writes that "our remote ancestors had not the slightest notion that such a thing as communicating ideas and feelings to someone else was possible." I found this absolutely fascinating, that perhaps our desire to make sound is just part of us. In this day and age of impressing others on social media or trying for hit songs, could it be that we have glazed over the most important, innate function of our voices — to just *be*?

I thought about childbirth, which I would experience at age 34 and again at 37, and how low guttural noises worked in tandem with my body's natural ability to bring a child into the world. To prepare for my first child's birth, I used hypnotherapy to enter labour in a state of relaxation, which helped with the early contractions. After being induced and beginning to fully experience the intense pain of labour, I asked for an epidural only to be informed that the person who administers them had stepped away to Tim Hortons for a coffee and doughnut. I was told I'd have to endure without anything other than nitrous oxide to relieve the pain. One woman's donut is another woman's dang-it.

Despite missing out on an epidural and embracing the spiritual experience of childbirth, I'm not sure how I would have weathered such an intensely painful experience without being able to groan and moan in low, deep tones pushed straight from my core, up through my lungs and throat, and out my mouth. Birthing and making sound went hand in hand. Birthing and making sound made everything easier.

History suggests that all along, when it comes to singing and using our voice, we wanted to emulate nature. Unlike bones dug up in the earth that give clues to how we and other creatures roamed the earth long ago, the larynx, our precious voice box, possesses no such evidence thanks to its composition of all muscle tissue — something that doesn't keep very well in the earth over centuries. Some researchers of Neanderthals, however, have found traces of the fragile hyoid — a C-shaped bone above our larynx — suggesting that this bone may have changed shape when our vocal cords evolved over time. Perhaps humans 1.8 million years ago possessed the ability to sing, but we can't be sure. We know from Egyptian notation that music was sung together by humans in religious and social situations, and this idea might confirm that hundreds of thousands of years ago, singing had become a social and bonding experience. This makes it that much easier to understand why we get a high from singing with others in modern contexts. Could modern ensembles such as Choir! Choir! Choir! which are built on open participation, as well as other community choirs, workplace choirs, and virtual ensembles be modern versions of these ancient musical gatherings? Humanity and society have shifted drastically, but the human heart and body might get the same rush today as they did in Greece in the early second century AD — you know, when they got all up in each other's zones and threw down some pretty dope hymns of the Mesomedes.

Chanting and exploration of various vocal registers is evidenced through graphic art of the Middle Ages, and as time progressed, a more harmonic presentation of voice and music came to be in the Baroque period. How extraordinary it must have been to hear music in more harmonic tonality after the medieval and Renaissance periods, when music was characterized by what we might perceive as discordant. Soon, opera was born and introduced the fusion of dramatic text with singing, which opened the floodgates for even more forms of expression through voice and performance.

SOUND AND VISION

Nellie Melba was an Australian operatic soprano. One of the most famous singers of the late Victorian era, she ditched the after-effects of an unsuccessful marriage and moved to Europe and found fame as a singer. She eventually debuted across the pond at the New York Metropolitan and is featured on the $100 Australian bill. Famously, Melba said these wise words: "The first rule in opera is the first rule in life: see to everything yourself." This advice is more poignant than one might think, considering we, with our instrument on us, and the choices we make in body and mind being instrumental to our success, really are seeing to everything ourselves. When Melba travelled to Europe, she further honed her natural talent for singing by studying with Mathilde Marchesi.

Marchesi's slow and steady approach led several singers of the day to unrivalled success. Marchesi also frowned upon a method of singing that required the singer to "smile" when performing, calling it absurd. She committed to an agile and precise technique of singing, although she maintained that she did not teach the bel canto method.

Bel canto, however, is more of a style than a method. The words themselves are Italian for "beautiful singing" and through the ages, the term *bel canto* has been dragged through many interpretations and descriptions, ultimately resulting in a whole lot of confusion.

The characteristics of bel canto are many, but the ones that truly matter involve matching singing tone and human emotion, the way the body can enhance vocal performance through gestures and relaxation, an emphasis on building muscle and clarity of tone, and a slow, steady practice. Adopted, these characteristics of the bel canto method will result in a wholly better voice. Another important detail to note is that the music that bel canto singers sang involved long held notes and often big, open Italian vowels, which required legato singing, or smooth singing. This brings me to the second most powerful concept I learned, after low breathing. From Mitch, I learned an aspect of singing, similar to legato singing, which made a gigantic difference to strengthening my voice. I learned to focus the sound in a forward, solid tone — a concept Mitch calls "line and movement." **Secret No. 16: Focus the sound.**

"Line and movement" or "creating a solid tone" is best shown through in-person or video instruction, so I encourage you to head over to emmgryner.com/videos and watch my video on it. Often, when we sing or do our warm-ups, we approach high notes with a sense of "yikes, here it comes!" or "scary high part approaching!" When we go for the higher notes, our eyebrows go shooting up to the sky, our eyeballs bulge, and our minds tell us to feel afraid, feel very afraid. We tense up our jaw and our facial muscles to somehow control the sound, as though that might make it all work out. When we're starting out and singing notes that we perceive as high or difficult, it's important to **do the opposite of what your body intuitively wants to do**. Singing high notes, for example, requires less tension, less control, and more relaxation. I'm going to say it again: do the opposite of what your body wants you to do. Imagine jumping out of the plane at ten thousand feet and, instead of tensing up, just letting go. Wouldn't that be better?

This sense of line and movement and of developing a solid tone will help you direct the sound as you relax. Still not making sense? It's okay. I talk more about this in Chapter 19.

I mentioned childbirth a few paragraphs ago. Anyone who has been through it knows it is not a "grab some cheese puffs and settle in for the show" type of activity. However, I found when I did relax into the pain, I was much better at handling it than when I didn't. I knew that if I tensed during contractions and pushing, the pain would have been far worse. Yup, the pain was undeniable. But I would have gone from an observer of this miracle to a hospital patient totally out of control.

I use childbirth as an example not because singing is painful (nor does it yield a cute baby and years of poopy diapers), but because it can be a frightening time, and in frightening times, the body has a natural tendency to tense up. Singing well, like most things we endure as humans, requires us to relax. Not just at practice time, not just in performance, but when we are pushing ourselves in our warm-ups to hit the high notes, form awkward new vowel sounds, and sustain long notes. From the first moments of preparing to sing, relaxation is so vital.

When we realize the link between our natural desire to sing, and the undeniable way nature itself just unfolds and allows all things to happen, we gain a stronger sense of the positive effects of letting go.

ACTION ITEMS

1. **Write down a time in your life when your voice helped you become more powerful, either physically or emotionally.** What were the effects of using your voice this way, both negative and positive? What are ways to ensure your voice is used positively?

2. **Refer back to your answers from Action Item 1 at the end of Chapter 6,** where you named times in your life where you were your most relaxed. **Reflect on these answers and expand on them** this way: How can you channel relaxation into preparing to sing? Consider visualizing as you breathe and get ready for warm-ups. Consider mind-body exercises to connect this relaxing vision and feeling to a physical action (for example, putting your index finger and thumb together when you are at your most relaxed state and resting your palm on your diaphragm as you tune into your belly breathing). You'll be able to train your brain to associate relaxation with preparing to sing.

3. Who do you love to sing with? This could be a choir, other people in your community, or a friend. It could be as easy as having a karaoke night with pals. **Make a non-negotiable appointment or schedule an event where you can have the experience of singing with others.** Notice any feelings it brings up for you, and write them down.

CHAPTER 13

LETTING GO

*"You may not control all the events that happen to you,
but you can decide not to be reduced by them."*
— MAYA ANGELOU

"Jam, woo woo . . . Rebel, that's right! . . . I'm on my own, I'll call my own shots . . . Thank you . . ." Ten-year-old me sang the song "Control" into a toy microphone in the luxurious privacy of my own bedroom, where I could dress up like the person I was emulating — Janet Jackson — and pretend I was giving the whole world a giant half-Asian, half-Canadian middle finger.

From the earliest days, we fight to have control, because believing we have it makes us feel like we know what's going on and that tragedy is not going to screw with our lives. With all of our ducks in a row, we can work on all of the other stuff that needs to be done, but the minute something that we don't like happens to us, we feel like the sky is falling. The fact is life is chock full of things that we don't —

and won't — like. I remember when I was dealing with the abusive fan, Joni telling me that "life isn't fair." When she delivered that news, she was like a shark opening up her jaws to a little tadpole, and I just swam in little circles croaking in despair, like I had never considered those words before: *Life isn't fair.*

Because I lived for a long time with the illusion that I was controlling my life, I found myself quite ill-equipped to deal with all of the hardship that hit me later on. I felt, quite frankly, the opposite of Janet Jackson circa 1986. I was freaking out of control. When things began to "happen to me" — like being dropped from the label, or getting stalked, or being left out of the next round of Bowie's band — I had no clue how to reckon with this feeling of losing control.

As a singer, it's extremely important both mentally and physically to embrace the concept that you are not in control.

In my talks with my friend, astronaut Chris Hadfield, when I asked him about stress and fear, which are directly related to control, he said that on his missions in space he had to come to terms with the fact that anything could happen. There are simply too many variables that he, Chris Hadfield, a mortal human, could not control despite years of military training, flying fighter jets, and preparing to become an astronaut. But he did say there was one thing he could control, and that was his attitude on his journey.

Eventually, I, too, began to see that relinquishing control had its benefits. **Letting go allows you to feel liberated, and it allows your voice to open up.** So as you approach high notes or long passages in music, just let go and see what amazing, powerful results come. Yes, you guessed it, it's **Secret No. 17: Let go.**

SICKNESS

One thing that every singer wants to be in control of is their health. I've outlined a few basic ways to start being healthy in your life as a singer, but just as an astronaut can't control what happens in space (or even on Earth), we sometimes cannot control the reality that part of being human means facing sickness. And sometimes, you have to sing through it. How does anyone do this? How do you know you're too sick to sing? Can just being upbeat allow you to make it through a performance?

It was October 1999. I wiped my nose on the set of *Saturday Night Live*. Stress and jet-setting all over the globe had furnished me with a nasty cold, conveniently, just in time for our highly anticipated late-night performance where we were going to sing two songs on live TV with Bowie. This was not the first time that I'd be plagued with a cold as a singer, but it certainly was one of the most unwanted.

I loved *SNL*. All of its trademark humour and wacky political skits were embedded in me from my adolescence. My brothers and I would constantly recycle the jokes from skits like "Toonces the Driving Cat." We loved anything Will Ferrell or Molly Shannon ever did. Yes, it was a big deal to be a small-town kid on this NBC set, smack dab in the middle of Manhattan, the centre of it all. And it sucked to be sick.

In recent years, illness has taken centre-stage thanks to the global pandemic that is COVID-19. If nothing else, the shock that accompanied the dangers of this disease and the precautions that every human on the planet was forced to heed proved to us that humanity can be hit with anything at any time, whether we are prepared for it or not. The fallout of this pandemic is certainly major — it is emotional, economic, political — in short, it has been the greatest blindside of our generation at the time of writing this book. This chapter is not meant to suggest how we may be able to happily skip through the meadows of life as terminal illness or ravaging diseases for which we have no cures find their way to us. Although there are countless instances where a song, a singer, or a magical musical moment healed someone's spirit and, in some cases, their body, I acknowledge that when our health is seriously compromised, life, in many ways, grinds to a standstill. Survival and, if you are lucky, recovery become all that matters, and singing — karaoke nights, carefree concerts, singalongs at bars, and whatever else — takes a backseat. But sometimes, the voice can guide us through. Even in the middle of a global pandemic, evidence of singing's saving grace was all around us. Songs sung in final hours, musicians coming up with any and every way to keep singing together, people who had never sung finally taking singing lessons and university music students making face coverings with more space so that choir members could breathe, sing, come together.

But how do you sing through illness? Let's take the common cold, for example, since it has been prevalent for so long and has plagued singers for eons. With no cure in sight, the common cold remains a major obstacle to functioning normally — speaking, working, maintaining a healthy energy level, and so on. When my students contact me and say they have a cold so they can't do their lesson, I say, "Show up anyway!" I encourage them to keep their lesson so that we can work out ways to sing through this nagging problem.

In 2017, I had booked a series of shows for myself around Ontario. They were all to happen in November of that year, in quaint theatres in towns that had special meaning to me. I assembled a great band, and we began rehearsing. As I approached the first of four dates, I came down with a severe chest cold. With two kids in my care who were going to school and me buzzing around town doing a million errands a day, it is no surprise that I came down with it. But it wasn't a little cold; it had a vice grip on me. I had the kind of cold that grasps your lungs, zaps your energy, has your nose flowing like a tap, and makes you feel like dog doo-doo.

My shows were sold out. My voice was almost gone. I texted Mitch, panicked.

He got back to me quickly. Mitch talked me down from the ledge and reminded me to approach my shows like I was an injured athlete. He assured me that the concert wouldn't be perfect, to my ears anyway, but I could make it through. Mitch's support relaxed me and reminded me that I've been through this before and I just had to follow what I knew would work.

So, what does work?

Like anything else, you need to assess what's going on rationally. Because only you know your body, you will know what works and what doesn't, and the more you get out there and sing through sickness, the closer you'll get to

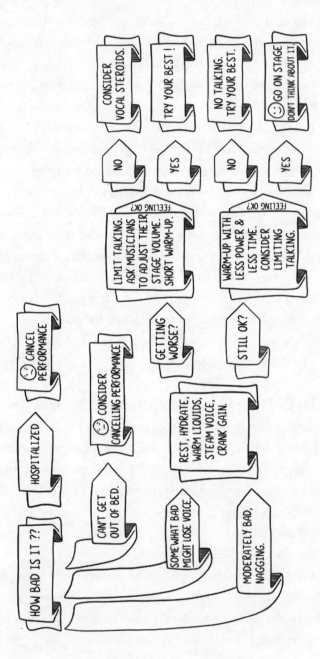

figuring that out. Mind you, every cold or flu is different, but here is a flow chart that shows the thought process I have when I am faced with having to sing through sickness:

I ended up playing all four shows with the help of tea, rest, extra gain on my mic, and steroids. I didn't have to cancel anything, and although I wasn't 100 percent and I couldn't deliver the way I really wanted, I was able to give something decent. In cases when illness is even more severe, sometimes you just have to ask yourself, What's the worst that happens if I have to cancel? Life will go on, and, sure, people will be disappointed, but at the end of the day, the world is not going to burst into flames because you had to cancel a few shows.

MORE WAYS TO LET GO

Nellie Melba was a woman who knew about letting go. "It is easy to sing well, and very difficult to sing badly!" she said. "How many students are really prepared to accept that statement? Few, if any. They smile, and say: 'It may be easy for you, but not for me.' And they seem to think that there the matter ends. But if they only knew it, on their understanding and acceptance of that axiom depends half their success. Let me say the same in other words: In order to sing well, it is necessary to sing easily." She knew about this a hundred years ago and how letting go and singing with ease was the answer to all.

What follows are a few ways to help yourself sing with ease.

Yoga

I call the time I was living in upstate New York my hermit years. Before I moved into an apartment, I lived in a poorly heated coach house on the side of a mountain, virtually invisible to all of humanity. My landlords were Holocaust survivors and former magazine writers. At a time in life when most women are out exploring the world, I drove my car all around the Catskills, surveying the beautiful landscapes, travelling aimlessly, and letting my mind be both full and empty. Under the shelter of ancient trees and old mountain ranges, I purposely refrained from meeting new friends, instead preferring to explore the world alone. While living in upstate New York, I decided I would begin a yoga practice. Learning yoga allowed me to expand a body that was wrapped up tight in wishing, confusion, childhood angst, and youthful curiosity. **Yoga was my first introduction to letting go, an approach that changed my singing forever.**

My dad had always done a form of yoga. Every night before bed, to alleviate back problems, dad would curl up like an egg on the carpet beside his bed and flatten his back slightly into the floor. He'd wrap his knees into his chest, hold that position, and do other things, all of which seemed normal to me. "I'm doing my back exercises," he would say. Mind you, Dad wasn't doing handstand scorpion or wounded peacock or any fancy yoga moves, but his simple practice benefitted his health for years.

You can explore the benefits for yourself, in a class, following a video, or with books, but however you approach yoga, the science is irrefutable. Along with the obvious physical benefits — increased flexibility, more muscle strength, improved blood flow, and so on — the mental benefits are enormous. Changes to the nervous system aid in stress relief, memory function can improve, and problems with addiction and focus can be nearly eliminated. The biggest gain of having a regular yoga practice as it relates to singing is in creating more space for the lungs to expand.

Therefore if relaxation is a major aspect of singing, then yoga is one of the quickest routes to getting there. You may be surprised to learn **Secret No. 18: Stretch yourself**. I mean this quite literally. Stretching your body, and then extending this to stretching the face, neck, shoulder, and upper body muscles will make a massive difference to your singing. You can explore my videos featuring some more stretches that will help your singing practice at emmgryner .com/videos.

Release Tension in the Jaw

Social media has its traps, but I've been known to use Twitter to invite myself into the bands of people I admire. I invited myself into Sass Jordan's band some years ago. A raspy, enigmatic rock 'n' roll singer — a sort of love child of Janis Joplin and Chris Robinson — Sass was one of my idols growing up. Her album *Racine* was a classic, every song a rock 'n' roll masterpiece.

So when I joined her band as a tambourine shaking backing singer, long after my days with Bowie, it was just a fun thing to do. Little did I know I was about to learn about letting go in a way that I could not have planned for.

Although Sass has played festivals with thousands and thousands of people in the audience, the shows I played with her were smaller clubs in tiny bars. We played all her hits from the '80s and '90s, and I was in musical heaven.

As I watched Sass perform her songs, her blond hair swaying back and forth, bracelets jangling and flowy black chiffon blouses flapping like flags in a warm Louisiana wind, I realized how different she was from me. She didn't give an eff about what anyone thought. She wore what she wanted, she knew what shoes to wear while singing (nothing uncomfortable), she knew not to constrict her diaphragmatic area so she could belt easily, and as she moved through all of her hits, I saw something quite amazing.

Sass was open. In all ways. Her body was open to the audience, her arms often outstretched, and her face as she sang was wide and giving. She opened up so huge that every ounce of sound could come out, yet she also just appeared so natural. I wondered how she could do this. I had never seen anyone sing this way. Not even David.

I started to analyze the way I sang, and I noticed that I held tension in my face. I held even more tension in my jaw. I watched videos of myself singing, and I noticed the tightness. Now, I recognize that tightness as fear. A fear of letting go. A fear of being judged. Sass has no fear of being judged, and therefore she could be rock 'n' roll, open, expressive, and generous. I learned so much from Sass in just a few short shows, about opening up my instrument. **When it doesn't come naturally, and when you carry fear,**

you need to make a conscious decision to let it go. Let go, and stretch.

I Know

Another way to let go is to simply accept that we don't know everything. As we age, we assume we know all there is to know. We tell ourselves that our age and experience is enough, we say things like, "It's not my first rodeo," which is not only unhelpful if we want to learn a new craft and be great at it, it's also something that old men presidents have said. Why would you want to say what an old man president has said?

One of the most inspiring words to me is "curiosity." Being curious about life, music, and love is one of the best ways to keep growing, because we see everything as an opportunity to learn. Saying "I know" can be a surefire dead-end to all the gifts curiosity can bring. From my time with David, I noticed his immense curiosity. From the unusual fashion choices I would bring to the band to this new world called the internet, from the songs of new indie bands to what could be explored next in art and music. A man who changed the world, who you might argue was an authority on all things music and fashion, was equally as curious about art long after the peak of his fame.

ACTION ITEMS

1. **Have a plan for singing through sickness.** Make a checklist of a few things you might need to get through a cold. Get those things now because

you won't want to when you feel like crap. Tea, steamers, lozenges, a towel — all things to have at the ready.

2. **Video yourself singing to identify where you hold tension.** Then find a way to incorporate stretching into your life, whether it's yoga, fitness, or more stretching before your warm-up.

3. **Watch other singers.** What do they do to let go and open up? Make this fun. Watch some concert footage, go to shows, organize a fun night where you screen a music movie. Or invite yourself into someone's band and steal all of their mojo.

CHAPTER 14

FAILURE IS GOLDEN

*"Hardships often prepare ordinary people
for an extraordinary destiny."*
— C.S. LEWIS

A LATE-LIFE FAIL

Later in life, when I began to be invited to speak to groups about my story, it was easy to be slightly terrified of the new opportunity but bury it under the illusion that I knew what I was doing. Speaking versus playing concerts? Well, I figured speaking to people was just the same as giving a concert, minus the music. How hard could it be? I told myself those two little words, *I know*, but this time it was accompanied with an annoyed, self-assured tone and that hand wave — *you* know the one, where it looks like you're waving a fly out of your face, beyond fed-up?

One afternoon a few years ago, I was invited to give a talk to a group of human resources experts at a luncheon. I was asked to talk about my story in music and share what

I had learned. The event was at a golf course near my house, and I figured, it's a local event, I'm cool — I'm going to dress like, well, a human resources expert, and I'll just wing it.

When I showed up, I realized I was going to really have to wing it because I had forgotten my laptop, which contained my notes and the slides I'd have played to support my talk. There was no time to go back to my office for it, so in desperation, I grabbed my acoustic guitar, which just happened to be in my car. Thought process: "Bingo! I'll serenade the ladies who lunch!" After all, my performances always wowed people, and I figured I'd just rest on that ability that I've cultivated over two decades, and everyone will go home happy. Before the talk began, knowing full well I was ill-prepared, I hid away in a back room and made last-minute notes, trying to avoid people.

Making a grand entrance has served me well as a musician. I heighten audience anticipation by making myself scarce before the show and conserving energy. But on that day I noticed the opposite was happening. I didn't get to know anyone's name in this small lunch group. I didn't get to hear anyone's stories beforehand or find out what anyone did at their company or what was even on the menu. As I took my place in front of the group, carrying my guitar and receiving minimal applause over green starter salads, it was as though I had been beamed in from another galaxy. Awkwardly, I started to realize that in forgetting my laptop, having no PA system to sing through, no slides, no real outline for the talk, and no sense of who was in the audience, I was essentially digging my own public-speaking grave. As I spoke, a deep sense of unworthiness infused my words, and, plagued by distraction, I knew I was failing at sharing my message. As I got deeper into my talk, I could tell that the group desperately wanted to hear me, to learn from me, but because I was unprepared and, therefore, unconfident, the whole thing tanked. Not to mention they'd probably seen a lot of speakers by that time in their careers, and they probably knew an effective one from an ineffective one.

So I had an epic fail. But **failure is merely an opportunity to change, to reframe, to start again**. And so I give you **Secret No. 19: Failure is an opportunity.**

SECOND CHANCE

At my next talk, I was determined to have a different experience. I equipped myself with advice from professional speakers and books on speaking, and I looked into how to best prepare for a presentation. I learned about ways to make a talk engaging, from body language to humour to focus and passion. I did my full vocal warm-up before speaking. I hired my sound technician to come and engineer the audio, which also included key performances of songs that would help tell my story. I went to the venue multiple times to look at the stage and audio system, to try out my slides. I asked the organizer to tell me who was going to be in the audience — what was the range of ages of the attendees, would they be male, female, trans, or other — and what they were hoping to take away from the talk. I probably don't have to tell you how successful that talk was.

Preparedness. We often associate a zest for life and all the opportunities it can bring with being young. After all, when we were young, it was totally fine to go out and get a crappy job to support our dreams. There was no shame in asking for help from those more experienced, opening our minds to learn anything and everything we could about our craft. Perhaps the message we can take away from this is not that we need to go and get a crappy job late in life to support a wild dream, but that we need to tell ourselves what we did when we were young, that anything is possible and there's no shame in trying stuff out. As we age, we amass wisdom, experience, and knowledge, but we're not as willing to be curious, to try something new and be okay with messing up sometimes.

When it comes to your own creative work, know that you have a story, one worth telling, and only you can tell that story properly. Energy can be felt, and preparedness is an energy with which no one can argue. Age has nothing to do with it. Simply prepare to give back and watch the most amazing sparks fly.

PREPAREDNESS: VOCAL EDITION

Earlier in the book, I talk about being prepared and how it can set you up for having your dreams come true. Well, once those dreams are coming true, **there is a practical aspect to being prepared** that I learned over the years. As a singer, you will want to do everything in the most professional way you can.

Before going into any situation where you will be singing publicly, it is worthwhile to familiarize yourself with the lay of the land. Even if you feel like you don't need to know this stuff, find it out anyway because the fewer surprises you have on the day of performing, the more you can focus on singing and enjoying the moment.

This list can help prepare you for any situation in which you are singing or using your voice:

- Where am I going?
- How am I getting there?
- Where do I park? Does it cost anything?
- How many people will be there?
- What ages will be there?
- How long do I have to sing for?
- Will there be a sound system?
- Will there be someone to run the sound system (if applicable)?
- What microphones are available (if applicable)?
- What does the stage look like? How big is it?
- Is there a room where I can warm up and relax?
- How big is the room (if applicable)?
- Is food provided, and if so at what time? For how many performers?
- If a meal is not provided, what provisions are there for food?
- Can my guests attend, and if so how many?
- What wardrobe is suitable for this event?
- Can I sell merchandise? If so, is there somewhere to do this? Will a table be provided?
- Who else will be performing at the event and when? For how long? What is the order of performers?

- Who will pay me at the end of the performance?
- How much have I agreed to charge for this event? Has a deposit already been sent? Does anything remaining need to be collected at the event?
- Who do I thank at the end of the event?

These questions are all part of a process called "advancing a show." You can do this work yourself, or you can have someone help you get this information. As you get further down the road, a manager will likely get all of these details for you, freeing you up to focus on the creative part of the show. You'd be amazed at how smoothly your performance goes when these details are provided for you and you didn't have to get them yourself or deal with the leaking energy of lingering questions. Sadly, as up-and-coming singers we often have to fight to get this information. Even musicians operating at a moderately successful level can still encounter people who think of performing as a fun little hobby, not a profession, so details can be hard to come by. Another reality is that people who invite you to sing are dealing with their own long list of preparations. They're not thinking of your needs 24/7. **Be bold enough to ask for what you need to know and the whole dang thing will go better for everyone.**

Being prepared is also a mindset — it's going into a performance ready to give your all in a focused, entertaining, and unique way. I remember watching Bowie before he would step onstage. In the wings of any stage in the world, he seemed to transform into another person. He went from approachable to untouchable. In this persona, David seemed to grow a foot taller. He became the largest version of himself. He was this from the moment he left his dressing room to the moment he walked back into it. Onstage, he was the person everyone loved to see perform — unpredictable, warm, funny, a hundred people in one, playing a part, enjoying the moment — a legend.

There are also big picture ways to be prepared for your life as a singer, which we'll explore in the upcoming chapters. For example, how will you run your business as a singer? What message do you want to send? What will your life as a singer look like? These questions should take you back to your vision board. In a few chapters more, we'll talk about another form of letting go, which is getting rid of negative energy in your life. So hard to do, but so worth it.

ACTION ITEMS

1. **Make a checklist for preparing for gigs.** Use the list in this chapter as a starting point to develop a way to be prepared for all of your events. Ask yourself — what do I need to know so I feel impeccably prepared for any event? Being impeccably prepared leads to better singing, and lots of good vibes.

CHAPTER 15

MAKING IT A BUSINESS

"I never dreamed about success. I worked for it."
— ESTÉE LAUDER

"You make a living at that?" is one of the most popular things I am asked as a musician. You get asked about something enough, and you start to laugh at it, but the question about whether or not singing my own songs can buy me a Healthy Choice microwavable linguini became more interesting and less annoying to me as I got older. I became intrigued that people really could not believe that music paid my bills. Why? Did they see music as a hobby? Did they think I got a free pass to just keep being a teenager through my thirties and forties? As I had babies and eventually became a single mom, what did they think then?

Singers and musicians all over the world are plagued by people poking holes in our ability to have a career in music. The funny thing is, I wasn't always professional. I had given the impression that I was a fiercely independent artist running my own show and operating my own label, but nothing could have been further from the truth, and in 2008, life caught up with me.

One day, I got a phone call from the government. Anytime the government calls you, you can pretty much bet they're not calling to shoot the shit and see how you're making out with your macrame hobby. The Canada Revenue Agency contacted me to question my legitimacy as a working musician who made a fair income. When the government doesn't believe you, it results in a woman in a three-piece suit bounding into your home with an industrial-sized laptop and a big frown on her face. Before we'd even said hello, this investigator was looking around my house at everything I kept, from art on the walls to paper towel roll holders, judging my every possession and interrogating me as though she wasn't CRA but CIA. This woman was so thorough in her questioning and her examination of my life, I worried that I was about to be rectally rehydrated in a dark room and have my limbs broken while the Spin Doctors' "Two Princes" played on repeat at 200 decibels. Yes, I was being audited.

I reviewed what could have possibly brought the CRA to my door. Could it have been the over $25,000 in taxes when I got my record deal which slimmed down to next to nothing the next year, after I got dropped? Was it that I had done business all over the world with a rock legend, and then the next year been cut from his band resulting in paycheques of a completely different calibre? Whatever it was, I was pissed off. I had lived with what so many musicians, artists, and young entrepreneurs had for so long — the dreaded "variable income." That means I could make thousands in one month, but practically nothing the next. Royalties, touring, and inconsistencies in activities are all normal for a musician. But to the regular person who works a nine-to-five, has a pension and benefits, not only is it unfathomable that anyone can survive this way, it's often deemed downright irresponsible.

What followed was an extensive review by CRA of every area of my life, and a digging up of about a million receipts. They suspected I had not been forthcoming about my income for a period of three years and informed me I had to repay $50,000 immediately. As an indie artist, I was blindsided. And it was me against the man, an ant looking up at Everest.

Now the unprofessional part of my life was not that I had actually hid income, it was that I was disorganized. I had been jet-setting all over the globe, writing songs, doing my thing, and failed to see how I needed to run my business in an organized way, detailing income impeccably and understanding all the ins and outs of my own money. Because I was so busy, my mom had offered to do my taxes every year. She sometimes worked on my filings with Michael Woods, who had been accountant to several Toronto bands with record deals, but I was removed from most of the process. Mom was kind enough to tally up all my receipts, but once the government got involved, it was clear that receipts didn't line up with reporting. This is where I went wrong. I wasn't in touch with my money flow. This disorganized approach made it seem that I was hiding income. My mission then was to prove that I was honest, but it meant going back through tonnes and tonnes of receipts, tour dates, boxes, and emails, making phone calls, filling spreadsheets — you name it — to prove my case.

Just as this was happening, Michael Woods, someone who I knew would be key to my coming out of this mess a success, took a terrifying fall down his stairs at home. The after-effects of this accident resulted in several of his organs failing, and tragically he ended up passing away, leaving all of his accounting work with a partner whom I didn't know well at all. I was left with no one to guide me through the difficulties of this time.

What does this have to do with singing? A crapload.

Because guess how much singing and music-making I did at this time? Zero. All creativity grinded to a halt. There was no music in me. I was in survival mode.

MAKE IT OFFICIAL

Instead of becoming Master of Puppets, I became Master of the Excel spreadsheet. I painstakingly combed through every tour date for the past three years and examined every income and expense so that I could craft a new presentation for CRA that could be legitimately backed up. I hired a new accountant, another Michael (this one Wong). Michael Wong had been an accountant with Zomba Records and now was the money guru for Outside Music, my album distributor in Toronto. It was only because Michael cared and had the time that I got through this terribly challenging time. I learned that **in order to be taken seriously, an artist has to present their art as seriously as any other corporate**

business. My books needed to be in order, they needed to be clear, and most importantly, I needed to understand where every cent was coming from and going to. After all of our work, we travelled to the CRA offices in Hamilton and, in what seemed like a court date, we sat face-to-face with representatives. After we presented months and months of hard work and documentation, Michael helped answer questions that I wasn't equipped to, and the penalty was dropped from $50,000 to $2,000.

Of course, the reduction in the penalty was a victory. But the bigger victory, and where this becomes useful to you, is what I can pass onto you. I learned that by understanding my business fully, and treating my "fun songwriting hobby-turned-carefree-lifestyle" with professionalism, I felt empowered and free. For the first time, I could see, with joy and curiosity, where money was being spent and where it was being saved. I could see from year to year that I had the ability to make money, track it, and enjoy doing it. Making money and keeping track of it was no longer just something I shoved aside in favour of living in the moment. Money became interesting to me. I became a business person. **Secret No. 20: Run an honest business.**

Today, I am regularly in touch with my accountant and my manager, and I make sure all money matters are clear and well-documented.

YOUR TURN

Some of you may have started out with street smarts about money and business. I applaud you if you have because you are one step ahead of everyone else. For the rest of you who are learning to navigate your music as a business, know that living with a variable income and living as an artist is possible. There are countless books about how to move through life with a fluctuating paycheque. For those of you who are not that organized about money or are constantly seeing it as scarce, the shift begins, you guessed it, in your mind. You need not go through a painful audit or a bankruptcy or a state of perpetual poverty to turn your music career into something prosperous and joyful. Just get on top of it. And at the root of getting on top of it, is shifting your mindset away from being scared of money, or thinking you'll never have enough of it.

After I turned my finances around, I entered one of the most lucrative decades of my career. Once I didn't have to worry about the disorganized state of my money, I was able to free myself to write more songs and sing more freely. Around the time of the audit, I made an album called *Goddess*. It was self-produced, charged with emotion, and cathartic, what with songs titled "Killing Spree" and "Empty Hole." The album I made next was a joyful pop album called *Northern Gospel* which spawned the sleeper hit "Ciao Monday." My voice blossomed on this album, with lush drawn-out harmonies on the song "Transatlantic" and a Canadiana-tinged ode to an expat called "North." This link between relaxing into my life (I had also become a mom to my son around then) and the openness of my voice was visible and audible to so many people. I began to do more shows, and soon I participated in something extraterrestrial that would make history.

If you can see running a business professionally as a gateway to opening your voice and having more freedom to create and grow artistically, you will be more inspired to make this part of your journey a priority.

ACTION ITEMS

1. **Get excited about the business of making music.** Whatever it takes to make it fun and to help you come across as more "together" is what you need to focus on. For some it may mean creating business hours that are non-negotiable. For example, from 10 to 12 o'clock, every day, I answer emails and generate a buzz about my music. When you don't have a boss, you have to be your own.

2. **Track your money in an organized way.** Make it a monthly pursuit or work with a bookkeeper to make sure everything is running smoothly. Track trends; see where you are spending maybe too much money or not enough. It is difficult to plan and live freely if you can't see what is coming in and out.

3. **Respect what you're doing.** If you've ever worked a proper job in your life, you know that you can't be late, you have to dress appropriately, and you have to work nicely with colleagues. If you would do that for someone else's business, why not for yourself? What you're making is just as important, if not more.

4. **Pay yourself a wage.** As musicians, we tend to take our cheques and pop them right in the bank, then take some money for ourselves. This hand-to-mouth way of living will eventually backfire. Work out a budget. What do you need to live? What can you pay yourself out of what comes in? Open up a business account and a personal account, and separate your transactions.

5. **Read, read, read.** Read books about money. Read books about variable income. But more importantly, read the books I mentioned earlier about changing your money mindset. Most money failures are rooted in bad attitudes we have absorbed over time. Just as you can will yourself to stay broke, you can will yourself to prosperity. Don't write off meditation and telling yourself mantras — they are incredibly effective tools to aid in money matters and shifting your mindset away for the idea of scarcity. There actually is enough money to go around, but you have to believe it.

CHAPTER 16

SURROUND YOURSELF
WITH STARS

*"Keep away from people who try to belittle your ambitions.
Small people always do that, but the really great make
you feel that you, too, can become great."*

— MARK TWAIN

"Hello, Emm, it's Chris Hadfield calling you from the International Space Station," was what came through the phone one morning in December 2012. It was just five months after I had given birth to my daughter, Aoife, and Chris sounded remarkably close by, though there was a slight crackle to the line and a very short delay. I smiled for two reasons: 1) someone was calling me from someplace other than planet Earth, and 2) because Chris tacked on "Hadfield" to his introduction that day, an odd choice for someone whom I had known for almost 15 years. I imagined Chris, 400 kilometres above Earth, floating weightlessly and doing routine phone calls back home, temporarily forgetting that we were on a first-name basis. Only this time, the call wasn't routine.

Chris and I both hail from Sarnia, Ontario, and our friendship began in the early 2000s when I wrote a song to commemorate his second spacewalk. "Christopher" is a classically infused pop piano ballad that captures what I imagine feeling weightless would be like, and it also celebrates the life's work of this dynamic man whom, at the time, I had yet to meet. The song contains one of my favourite lines: "we are just driving in cars / but Christopher walks on the dark." I'll never forget how Chris responded to hearing the song I wrote for him. He said, "Spaceflight is complex, dangerous, demanding — and magical. When I first heard 'Christopher,' it somehow captured all of that — the quiet aloneness, the contemplative emotion, and the powerful surge of actually being there. Emm's creativity got it just right, like the soundtrack to a spacewalk — when you steal a moment to deliberately notice where you truly are, weightlessly orbiting our world in wonder."

The exchange was enough to kick off a brilliant friendship. Chris and I began to get to know one another by occasionally duetting at concerts. He'd strum his guitar, and we'd play Canadian folk songs while harmonizing. A former military man and fighter jet pilot with a huge love for singing and playing music, Chris was and is always a magnetic person to be around. To hear from him — whether it was from space or from his cottage on St. Clair River that straddles the border between Ontario and Michigan — was always a joy.

Later in life, I discovered that he was actually born "Chris" not "Christopher," making his statement about my song, which never bothered to expose the foul-up, even more of a testament to his grace and kindness.

While on the phone that day in 2012, Chris told me that he planned to be in space for five months aboard the International Space Station, and during that time he wanted to collaborate on some music. "Sure," I said, holding my squirming baby daughter in one arm and the phone with the other hand, thinking, if your space bosses have not given you enough to do up there — sure, I would love to collaborate on music! Chris told me he wanted to record a cover of Bowie's "Space Oddity," the beautiful, ethereal guitar-laden classic from 1969, which tells the story of an astronaut's ill-fated mission into space, "far above the moon." Perhaps as a result of doing music independently for 20 years, and having my own staunch ideas on what people should do with their time, I tried to talk him out of it and suggested he record a lesser-known song called "I Took a Trip on a Gemini Spaceship" from the *Heathen* album. But Chris's vision — to do "Space Oddity" in space — was already solidified, and he wanted to know if I could help.

I felt open, and I really am fond of Chris. I also possess a life-long fascination with space exploration, so I agreed. In a small room in my house in my little town, I sat down at my keyboard, far below the moon, and plunked out an opening sequence to a new version of "Space Oddity." My intro began with the majesty of an F major seventh chord, arpeggiated and mellow, followed by an E minor seventh chord, equally as dreamy. These chords were played with a spirit that harkened back to another legendary song, one of my all-time favourites, Peter Gabriel's "Here Comes the Flood." I played through the entire song on piano, recorded it, and then sent it to Chris.

Communicating with someone in space is something to behold. In the first few days of them being up there, you receive an email from NASA. In it, you are instructed to send any emails for the space crew to an individual on the ground in Houston, Texas, who will then forward on to the recipient whatever you have written (no attachments over 3MB, please), wherever in the galaxy they happen to be. Strict guidelines are laid out by NASA: "be cognizant that email messages, whether they are from family, friends, co-workers, or the mission control and management teams, can affect the psychological well-being of the crew, so it is critical that all those sending messages to the crew understand the potential effect and ramifications of their messages. Your efforts to focus on constructive comments will go a long way in helping to achieve a pleasant environment for the crew during their space mission."

I've often thought this considerate directive should apply to all humans, whether they are floating around in space on a mission or just doing normal things here on Earth. That is to say, wherever you are: "Don't upset people with stuff that doesn't matter."

I sent my piano part to Houston and it went on to Chris on the ISS. In the days that followed, Chris loaded my piano version of "Space Oddity" into GarageBand. He then performed and recorded what I consider one of the most beautiful vocal performances I've ever heard him give. Somehow, orbiting Earth and experiencing weightlessness seemed to slightly alter Chris's vocal sound. He sounded light, carefree, and passionate.

He describes the experience, however, a little differently. "You can't get deep notes," says Chris, who spoke to me about singing for the writing of this book. "You don't get a full diaphragmatic expansion without gravity to help, and your sinuses are always clogged up because there's nothing to drain them. It's like standing on your head for three hours — everything's in the wrong place and all clogged up . . . but you can learn how."

There was another difference with this new version Chris and I were crafting. With the aid of Chris's son Evan, the lyrics to the tune were rejigged so that the astronaut in the new version makes it back to Earth safely: "Planet Earth is blue and there's so much left to do." Rewriting the lyrics to a classic rock anthem was a ballsy move, but Chris gave himself license to reimagine the song, and did it from a perspective that perhaps no one singing that iconic song would ever have again. When Chris sent the new version back, which contained my piano, his vocals, and the new lyrics, I was swept away. His performance seemed to dance perfectly atop my piano track. It was hollow yet rich and full of possibility and presence. His voice beamed back all the mysterious qualities of that unique location. To me, it was a match made in heaven.

Chris gently encouraged confidentiality on the project, stressing that it was a private, personal project, so I kept it under wraps. But the more I listened back, the producer in me emerged. The song needed more. I also had the advantage of knowing what Bowie's music was like with all the trimmings, the full band and everyone rocking. For David, more was, well, more, in the best way. I became convinced that this version required a little disruption, a little harkening back to the spirit of the original. It needed drums, bass, guitars — the whole treatment. It required the handiwork of someone who could build a rock track upon these two fragile yet dreamy elements — my piano and Chris's voice. But the stakes were high — this couldn't just be any rock track, this would have to be a rock track that would be able to stand beside the psychedelic, beloved original.

AMPING IT UP

At the time, I was working with a producer named Joe Corcoran on some of my own music. An affable ginger-haired chap a few years younger than I, Joe is a master of every instrument you could possibly imagine. What was more, he *got* Bowie. I knew Joe could transform a delicate ballad into something effervescent. The only thing was, he'd need to do it quickly, do it well, and honour the spirit of the 1969 song while making something brand new.

I typed Joe an email from my humble century house in St. Marys: *Would you help with this? There's probably no money in it.* Joe's response? *This sounds cool, a guy in space.* Accustomed to the unpredictability of the music industry, he accepted the challenge, not knowing if the project would ever really unfold.

Within a few days, Joe had tracked a breathtaking performance that was built around a bass distortion. Joe recalled the experience for this book. "For me the first thing that really clicked was the fuzz bass, because it was not the move that a regular music guy would do to a somber piano track, but for me that was the thing." Using ambient space station noises, which Chris had recorded and assembled on a SoundCloud page, Joe put the finishing touches on the track.

"I'm interested in pop music that's art, and when I was creating some of the sounds on the Chris Hadfield version, I was trying not to ape the Bowie version, but ape the attitude of the Bowie version," says Joe of the project, looking back. "I took it very seriously. I thought of the way some of Bowie's guitar players had elements of organized chaos. Like in 'Heroes,' Robert Fripp doing his weirdness going through the whole thing. I made a decision to commit to a level of weirdness." Joe's idea to mimic the spirit of the Bowie version worked. I suggested a few subtle changes, like some keyboard sweeps into epic parts of the song and the instrumental sections that set up the next verses, and Joe took it to the next level. It wasn't long before we had in our earthly hands a version of "Space Oddity" for Chris to hear. Now that all the instrumental parts had been refined and recorded, he would need to re-sing his vocal over everything to make sure it all lined up and sounded cohesive.

From the quiet of his sleep station with the door closed, Chris sang into a Sennheiser mic that he had wired into his iPad. He knocked it out of the park. Joe mixed the track, sent it back, and voila — "Space Oddity in Space" was born. Chris made plans to shoot a video of himself singing the song aboard the ISS.

Through this process, Chris was hoping to clear the song with Bowie and his people and also perhaps to receive

David's blessing. I had already sent an email to David telling him that an astronaut friend of mine from Canada was hoping to record his song in space. David thought the idea was thrilling, but I didn't hear much from him over the winter and spring of 2013.

By April, Chris's time as commander of the space station was coming to a close. In five months' time, Chris and the crew had set records for the amount of scientific research completed on ISS to date. They had upgraded the onboard data system to be significantly faster and more capable, for science uplink/downlink, and they had completed grapple and docking/undocking of the SpaceX Dragon unmanned cargo ship.

"Space Oddity" was the only song of Bowie's that he didn't own, so Chris proceeded to reach out to the people who did hold the rights, Songways. Although Chris had connected with Kathy Ostien at Songways, things were slow-moving. Chris felt strongly about wanting permission, and with only one month left in orbit, no one was getting back to anyone and time was running out. I also thought this was shaping up to be significant, and David better chime in. My email in May 2013 to David bore the very urgent subject line: *30 Days left in Space*. Whether it was that unusual subject line, or David suddenly had a small window of time in his very busy life, I'll never know, but he finally responded. *Can we get a sync licence for the astroman?* he wrote, cc'ing his business associates.

Chris's final days aboard the ISS were busy to say the least. In addition to preparing for the crew's return to Earth, an ammonia leak aboard the space station had just been detected. The leak threatened the health of everyone aboard the ISS, and presented the potential of having to abandon ship if they couldn't get it fixed. The song and video fell "way down the list," says Chris, in terms of priority. Expedition 35 crew members Chris Cassidy and Tom Marshburn were sent into the blackness to remove a 260-pound pump controller box that was said to be the source of the leaking ammonia coolant, and they replaced it with a spare in about three hours. The spacewalk and repair were a success. Despite this unexpected emergency hurdle during Chris's final days as space station commander, the song still remained an important part of his time there.

Wearing a casual T-shirt and some light socks, Chris shot a video of himself singing along to the song. As Chris sang and strummed his guitar in space, floating around in a way that Hollywood CGI could only dream of re-creating, you could feel his combined love for space and music. In other camera angles, he showed us magnificent starry views outside the space station window, and we got to see the look on his face as he observed the planet and the galaxy from this amazing, rare vantage point. As the chords shifted in their prog-rock, jazzy way, we were taken along on a trip in orbit, the lights of the Earth racing by from the heavens. We felt Chris's heart.

With video footage freshly edited together by Evan and east coast filmmaker Andrew Tidby, the experience was finally ready for the world to share. Just before Chris was set to return to Earth, the first music video shot in space was released.

MAJOR TOM

When the news hit, everyone from BBC to CNN were phoning me up, keen to know the story behind the release of this euphoric bit of footage. I had to ask my mom to come and watch my kids because the media attention was so intense and I found myself talking to the press morning till night. Outlets all over the world featured articles about the video and the song.

"A cover has rarely been this fitting," *Rolling Stone* magazine trumpeted.

The *New York Times* wrote, "The video . . . may have cemented [Hadfield's] reputation as the world's best-known singing astronaut."

In a *Globe and Mail* article, Brad Wheeler wrote, "The most significant shift from Bowie's original to Hadfield's reimagination has to do with context. The release of the single in 1969 coincided with the first Apollo moon landing — a Cold War expedition, by any other description. Hadfield's mission, on the other hand, was a joint one with Russian cosmonauts. Space and superpowers are now shared; and the stars look very different today."

By the week's end, I was exhausted and exhilarated; I couldn't possibly imagine how Chris felt.

Chris tells the story of coming back to Earth. "When I landed in Kazakhstan and the rescue forces were there, they opened the hatch and the guy who leaned in was a guy I knew, a Russian rescue specialist, and loudly, in Russian, he said, 'I saw your video clip, it's great!'" The video had only been released 12 hours prior to Chris's return to earth, yet the video had unified the world.

And then there was David.

With the stardust finally starting to settle, David wrote to me, sending one line that filled me with so much joy and gratitude: *This whole thing is so beautiful. Well done girl.* Publicly, he called it "the most poignant version of the song ever recorded," and I could imagine his smile and his boy-like wonderment watching the video from his penthouse in the Village. I knew it had been special to him.

Perhaps it doesn't matter how famous you are — if someone sings your song in space, you can't help but be overcome with joy and wonder. I witnessed the epic ability of music and singing to cultivate happiness, this time from an unexpected corner of the galaxy.

———

The gear used in this achievement was minimal, reinforcing that your own ideas, your experiences, and your circumstances surrounding music in your life can eclipse the need for expensive recording equipment. The fact that Chris, despite all kinds of physical compromises, felt inspired to sing and was fuelled by excitement about his environment and the magic of that iconic song also shows that not everything in your environment needs to be perfect for you to sing. I mean, his dang diaphragm wasn't even working the way it should.

FAST FORWARD

In 2017, almost four years after the release of the video and one year since David passed away, Chris and I found ourselves in New York City at a celebration of David's music. Old band members had come together, some with heavy hearts, to celebrate and perform David's music for an audience of fans who missed him greatly. We all gathered at Terminal 5, a box-like venue located in Hell's Kitchen, and three thousand adoring Bowie fans filled the industrial space. As the original version of "Space Oddity" was performed with powerhouse Gail Ann Dorsey belting it out, Chris and I stood next to each other poring over the stage from a balcony ledge. We gave each other knowing grins and a hug, a little bit chuffed that we had shared that experience of recording his song partially in space, partially on Earth. We had made the man himself smile a little bit over it all. As we stood side by side, we took in the evening's music like a couple of grateful kids from Sarnia, Ontario, who had each travelled vastly different paths, but because of music, shared a common bond.

"Space Oddity in Space" has received over 200 million views. Though it brought great recognition to everyone involved, none of us entered the project with the goal of success or making money. We simply stayed authentically open to the creative process, to making music, to hearing a human sing in space, to watching us all try something new and fun.

Of the experience, Chris told me, "When you go around the entire planet in an hour and a half, you suddenly realize it can't be very big. You can go around the whole thing in an hour and a half — it's small, it's finite. On Earth, we tend to exaggerate the distances and therefore the differences between ourselves, but when you go around that quickly, you realize Earth is just a small finite place and we're all in this together and the shared experience of being human outweighs everything else. The planet is just a little shared spot, the atmosphere so incredibly thin, the oceans incredibly shallow. Things like — the sheen of rain that's on a sidewalk — seen from a spaceship — it puts it all into perspective, its fragility and the fact that we're all in it together."

Secret No. 21: Surround yourself with stars.

ACTION ITEMS

1. **Surround yourself with people who excite and inspire you.** No further action is needed on this one. Just try it.

2. **Start seeing imperfection as perfection.** Gear, vocal ability, life demands, circumstances — very rarely will all of the elements align for you to work towards your goal. So focus on what does seem to be manageable yet inspiring, and go for that.

CHAPTER 17

THE BALANCING ACT

"Try something different. Surrender."
— RUMI

There is a YouTube video of a woman singing my song "Acid." It kicks off with the slightly frazzled woman saying "Mommy's singing right now" to her toddler daughter who is off-camera clamouring for her attention before she begins. The woman, who goes by the username Zovjraar, begins to sing over top of my recording, her voice drowning out mine. A mellow, wistful crowd favourite from 1998 in the key of A flat, "Acid" is about a dude from Coventry with whom I fell in love at age 21, who ran off with, as he called her, a "babe in a faux fur coat," leaving my heart in pieces. At the time of writing it, I really felt like I had lost a great romance and lost the world. The lyrics in the bridge, "Now I think I might get all 1967 on you / and run screaming to the balcony / but I can't do that, can't do / I gotta keep my good composure / And swallow everything I wanna say," reference the famous balcony scene from *The Graduate* where Dustin Hoffman's character hysterically interrupts his love Elaine's wedding, hollering her name from the second floor of the church and banging on the glass, much to the horror of all the wedding guests. I remember wishing I could do this, too, to get back the one I loved. In Zovjraar's video, she disappears blissfully into the song, glancing at lyrics now and again, and gazing out the window. By the song's end, she has transformed. Her entire body has relaxed, her face beams a smile of utter contentment. It's one of my favourite videos of all time. It is, quite simply, a very real example that singing can transform a person's state of mind and, in this case, a busy mom, who no doubt has a whirlwind of responsibility awaiting her when the camera clicks off.

Balancing work, family, personal life, and everything else is an ongoing, unrelenting struggle for many of us. So many of us feel that we are stretched thin, doing all of these things half-assed and not really able to imagine any other way of moving through life. We tell ourselves there is only one of us, and there are only so many hours in a day. As singers, this belief can really affect the way we perform, because stress and overwhelm can interfere with our ability to make sound. What's more is that singing can be the first thing to go when faced with a mountain of responsibility.

The other side of it all, however, is what singing can bring to a life that feels overwhelming. Just as Zovjraar transformed in the span of four minutes, music has the incredible power to change us and sometimes at lightning speed.

In the early days of having babies and doing music, I found the pull to be with them astronomical. I would literally finish my last note and have everything ready in my car to speed home because I knew they needed my body and my milk for nourishment. I would sometimes have them with me at a venue; other times, when I couldn't be there or have them with me, I'd pump bottles and bottles of milk. The learning curve of breastfeeding was steep and exhausting for me.

PUMP: NOT JUST AN AEROSMITH ALBUM

Six weeks after giving birth to my son, Ronan, I flew to Vancouver to perform at the Paralympic Games, an event that sees athletes with disabilities performing in all different sports. It was my first performance after becoming a mom, and how surreal it was to have this new, beautiful boy in my life, and then have to leave him to go to work. I had sung my entire life, but everything felt new now. I felt like I had a new purpose, like I was an entirely new person. I was still getting used to not having him in my body, and after a difficult run up to learning how to breastfeed, I had only recently got the hang of it. I was nervous about leaving him, even if I had just scheduled my trip to be a flying visit — there and back in about 24 hours' time. He was only feeding from me, not having formula, and his all-you-can-eat buffet was about to fly four thousand kilometres away. It could not have felt more wrong.

So I pumped. With my fancy Medela electric pump that they tried to design to look like a fashionable tote I filled many, many, *many* bottles in the days before leaving. I did well at the pumpfest and was able to leave Ronan about twenty mini-bottles of my milk, some of which went into the freezer and some into the fridge. And then I got on the plane.

No one told me what would happen next. By pumping like a maniac before I left, I had satisfied my concern that Ronan would have enough food while I was away, but I had created a terrible situation for myself, which I only realized at a cruising altitude of thirty thousand feet. My breasts grew to the size of cantaloupes on the plane, and the pain increased by the minute. Even though I had my pump with me, there was nowhere to really drain my rapidly expanding and aching chest. I couldn't pump in my seat because the sound was loud and it would have been really awkward to put a cone up to my breasts while some stranger was next to me. The bathroom was no place to do it, because I'd be in there the whole time, and as everyone knows there is hardly room to move. Getting the milk out would take 15 to 20 minutes minimum, and I knew if I pumped again, I'd also just be making the situation worse. My body would keep producing more milk rapidly. If you've ever been on a plane as a lactating woman, you know it feels pretty much like being shoved into a soup can while someone is squeezing your body from the inside with vice grips while laughing into your ear, "You, my dear, are going to explode, but first you will suffer incredible pain." Basically during the whole four-hour trip to Vancouver, I was in immense pain and there was nothing I could do about it. I had missed the chapter in *What to Expect the First Year* on pumping too much milk before jetting off to do a concert. Oh right, that chapter doesn't exist.

Once I landed and got to the hotel, I was able to relax and stretch out to pump. But the resources and comfort for nursing women out in public are still so minimal, not to mention the reactions of others to the act itself. Feeding our children from our bodies, one of the most natural things in the world, has its beauty and wonder devastated by the attitudes of society and the objectification of women. It was one of the things as a new mom that absolutely infuriated me. I remember seeing a nursing room at an airport in Alberta. It had fluorescent lights, one creaky old rocking chair, and nothing else. This wasn't where a woman could feed her child, this was a scene from *Rosemary's Baby*.

The baby years demand more of you than other parenting years, this is a fact. We are chemically and biologically tied to our children, and my best approach to balancing this with my career came by adopting two modes: preparation and surrender.

Before I gave birth, I finished my duets album *Gem and I*, and I also assembled a compilation album titled *The Best of Emm Gryner*. These albums were done in their entirety and the promotion was fairly complete before I had my son. In this way, I was able to roll out these two records with very minimal extra work. I also decided that I would surrender. As a busy-body with a need for control, this was challenging, but I realized that some things — tending to Ronan's cries, working on his sleep habits, and engaging with him — were going to be crucial to his development and knowing this allowed me to surrender with ease. The ability to adjust expectations was crucial in balancing work and personal life.

GET OVER YOURSELF

When I was 19 I joined a reggae band called Big Bamboo. It was not a typical move for me, but it was one of the most memorable projects I had been in, perhaps because the music was nothing like anything I had ever learned or written myself. The feel of reggae is completely different to straight-up pop. The beats fall in different places, and the way you move to it is the complete opposite of how you might move to "The Safety Dance" by Men Without Hats, for example. Learning all of Bob Marley's hits was quite an education, but a bigger education came for me when I had a heart-to-heart conversation with Altaf Vellani, a Kenyan-born percussionist who was in the band. We were discussing my musical dreams, and I was waffling on how to put together a band of my own and really see my songs come to life. Altaf said something to me that has stayed with me my whole life. He said, "You have to respect yourself enough to ask others to play with you."

Respect. I had never even thought about the concept of respect as a teenager. I mean, I knew I wanted to be adored. I wanted to be admired, celebrated, and recognized. But what Altaf was teaching me was that all of that would have to start with me. And **Secret No. 22: Ask for help.**

Asking for help is no different from asking others to play with you; just like new musicians, new parents need support. We need to know when we need to ask for help and just do it. It isn't weakness, it's recognizing that if we see ourselves as part of a community, made up of helpers and givers, healers and friends, our life's difficulties and demands can be made a little easier to endure.

SELF-CARE

Oh, self-care. Is it a bubble bath? Is it a glass of wine? Is it a 20-minute walk in the woods? It's funny what the world thinks women need to thrive. I prefer to see self-care less as a specific activity and more as prioritizing one's self. I was so crappy at this for so many years, and because of that, everyone around me suffered. I sacrificed my sleep for my kids, I made everyone's meals before mine, and, oh heck, I'll admit it — and you can too — sometimes my meals have been the grilled cheese crusts the kids leave behind on their plates.

A tried and true way to champion yourself is to review your values and your needs and figure out what should happen to really give those parts of your life attention. We simply can't feel fulfilled and creative if we can't get any sleep, for example. We can't help others feel healthy if we haven't had enough water and feel dehydrated. We can't love someone else if we aren't loving ourselves. We hear this all the time, yet we fail to heed the advice.

As a woman, I've felt that I need to fight relentlessly for time for myself. I need to schedule that time, keep it, and honour it as I would an appointment with a treasured friend. Balance comes so much more easily when you feel you have had that time for yourself.

Working on your warm-ups or developing musical projects can also be part of self-care. Sometimes we need to ask our partners for the space and time to be alone to work on creative projects. Sometimes we need to ask a babysitter to come, not because we need to do a host of domestic chores and errands, but because we want to go and do nothing for a little bit. We can give and give and give, but it won't be long before we have nothing left, and this trap is just too easy to fall into.

Recently, I looked around my house and realized that, holy shit, I don't have a desk set up for myself. I also realized, holy shit, I don't have a nice place to get ready in the morning. Holy shit, I don't have a quiet place to meditate. It was (wait for it . . .) about a *decade* into parenthood before I realized I didn't have and desperately needed those places for myself. So I made sure to create these niches, and I opened myself up to regular meditation practice and workouts. I was quicker to relax in difficult situations. This was a huge shift in balance. And as a single stay-at-home mom, no one was really helping me. I needed to meet my needs all on my own. Once I did, the whole house became a happier place.

There are countless books that might appeal to you on the topic of self-care. My personal favourite is actually a parenting book, called *The Conscious Parent* by Dr. Shefali Tsabary. By demystifying the way I looked at parenting, I was able to shift into self-care much more easily instead of getting caught up in parent-child power struggles. Dr. Tsabary's book was one of the most influential of my life.

GRATITUDE

Finally, gratitude. Even in the depths of despair, we have things to be grateful for. Moving through life from a place of true thankfulness, for even the little things, allows us to relax into our circumstances. **If we desire change in our**

circumstances, change is easier to make when we are grateful for what we have.

The best way I've found to keep gratitude at the front of my mind is by writing gratitude letters. I think of three people a day that I want to thank, and I write them a letter. Do I send this letter? Not usually. But I have sent a few. Writing down what we are thankful for, specifically and directly, can be much more powerful than just closing our eyes and imagining the things we are grateful for. That works, too, but for me, writing down words, seeing them on paper, categorically telling another human what you are thankful for makes it all the more real. Suddenly, the sense of "drowning in the day-to-day" becomes less pervasive. After some time doing this, you will remember what matters to you. And when you remember what matters to you and are grateful for what you have in your life, you're living your present, best life, no matter what else is going on.

ACTION ITEMS

1. **Identify where in your life you can ask for or accept help.** Refer to your answers from Action Item 3 in Chapter 11 (What are the needs you have to have met to shine?). **List the ways self-care can play a role in ensuring these needs are met.**

2. **Write gratitude letters** to three people. To really challenge yourself, write a gratitude letter to someone you don't believe deserves your gratitude. By pushing to find something to appreciate in someone difficult, even the smallest thing, you enable

the shift to become a more compassionate person. It's easy to be thankful for the nice people, but even (and especially) the difficult people in our lives can teach us so much about ourselves. Thanks, difficult people.

Part 4

THE
HOME STRETCH

CHAPTER 18

SINGING THROUGH DARKNESS

"1. You must let the pain visit.
2. You must allow it teach you.
3. You must not allow it overstay.
(Three routes to healing)"

— IJEOMA UMEBINYUO

The year was 2001. I was 26. When I was making my
Asianblue album in Los Angeles, I spent a good deal of time
with my brother Frank, who at that time was working exclu-
sively with Scott Humphrey (who had produced many rock
albums by artists like Rob Zombie and Mötley Crüe). A
painter from Canada had been invited to Scott's home to
create huge eight-by-ten-foot oil paintings for Scott's four-
thousand-square-foot gated manor. The painter, Sean, was a
blue-eyed, soft-spoken 25-year-old from London, Ontario.
Sean was tasked to transform the walls of the Hollywood
studio with his Giger-esque, dystopian, figurative art.
During a visit to the studio, I met Sean. As he helped tidy

221

the kitchen one day, I talked his ear off a mile a minute, while he nodded and said only a few words. It was a charming introduction.

A week or so later, at a barbecue in West Hollywood, Sean walked in with an old friend of mine. Dani was the boy who had ignored me on the bus ride when I was in grade school, and later, Dan, as he had come to call himself, became my friend and co-writer on *Asianblue*, penning the song "Lonestar" with me. Sean was dressed in long black pants and a long-sleeved black velvet shirt — an odd costume for anyone in California. I was intrigued. It turned out Sean was covering up the aftermath of tumbling into poison oak on a recent mountain bike expedition. Despite his fair skin being entirely covered in a hideous rash, he was jovial and present. We poured margaritas from the same pitcher and soon fell madly in love. And as if it were written into a Hollywood film script, the word *LOVE* is carved in caps into the cement at the foot of that house at Fountain and Fairfax. I don't think I noticed it on that day, but walking by it months later, it stared back at me, and it is still there now.

Love letters flew back and forth by email, and as we moved through this euphoric new feeling that neither of us had ever felt, we became best friends and lovers. As the world changed in 2001, neither of us could really understand what was happening, but we hung on tight to each other, watching the news — a couple of Canadians waking up in Scott's gothic, sprawling man-studio, finding certainty in only each other. I remember saying to Sean that all I ever needed was to make *Asianblue* and come home to him. Music and love consumed me.

The next year, on an autumn trip we took to England, under the ashen cover of Yorkshire skies, Sean proposed. He had been carrying an antique diamond ring in his luggage, nervous and excited to pop the question. I was completely surprised. Prior to this, I remember telling him on one midnight walk through Forest Lawn Memorial Park that we should never get married. I guess I thought that being "tied down" would take the romance out of what we had, but when he asked me that day, I knew I wanted to start a life with him as my husband.

The person I had fallen in love with was a leisurely artist who would lose himself in Peter Jackson films all day long and wear loose clothes covered in paint from his projects. The person he fell in love with was energetic and mischievous. I once made a scavenger hunt for him with a dozen romantic objects, all strewn through the Hollywood Roosevelt hotel, and giddily watched him uncover them. For one of his birthdays, I blindfolded him and surprised him at the end of a long drive, showing up at Big Bear, just a few hours outside of LA, where we stayed at some wacky theme cottages in the mountains.

This was me at that time — full of life, brimming with youthful ideas, and fresh off the Bowie tour. Possibility still swirled in me, to share my music, to dive into everything even if I didn't totally know myself and was still trying to process and decode my time with Bowie. As Sean's partner, I also wanted to see him share his art, and when he had an exhibit at a gallery in Beverly Hills, his mom flew in from Canada and I was the proud girlfriend.

We had moved back to Canada in 2002 and lived in the house in Montreal owned by Kate McGarrigle, who I loved being around. Kate was a sort of folk rebel and national treasure, and she and her sister Anna just did their own thing, having been through the music business in all its various incarnations. They made the music they wanted, but enjoyed life in Montreal immensely. Hearing their sweet blend of harmonies became part of the experience of being home. I imagined them upstairs, family heirlooms and beautiful antiques all around them, sipping tea or red wine while they rehearsed or wrote. I know that sometimes when I went away on tour, Sean would go up and see Kate. They would polish off a bottle of wine together, and trade stories. With close friends in cozy quarters, our time in Montreal was marvelous.

We returned to Ontario a few years later, to a quaint riverside town called St. Marys, population seven thousand. We rented a house and felt happy living closer to our parents. We were able to continue doing music and art while socializing with local friends. Our responsibilities were few, and I often view this time as "reverse retirement," doing nothing at all but still young and energetic.

—

In 2004, we married in front of 60 of our closest friends and family at an idyllic church on a lake in cottage country near Haliburton, Ontario, and we felt our love ripple through the congregation. "I wish I had what they had," one of Sean's cousins said to my manager at the time, Michael, who had rung the church bells, an appropriate move for an Irish-Catholic man from Limerick. We were pronounced husband and wife by a female minister wearing Doc Martens, and after kissing and strolling down the aisle, we tore away from the church to the sounds of Modest Mouse's "Float On" blaring from my black Honda Civic. My car, which had been lovingly decorated by my best friends with pink and white paper flowers, disappeared down a country road so Sean and I could have a quiet moment with each other to take in everything that had just happened.

Later at the inn where we continued the celebrations, our families mingled and danced; Sean's dad let loose, jiving around the dance floor with a tie wrapped around his head. Even Sean and I choreographed our own dance moves to "Solid" by Ashford and Simpson. Our performance was a sight to behold, two people with not a lot of rhythm trying to get soulful. Families united, we danced till almost dawn. After it all, Sean and I disappeared to a private cottage for some days alone, which we cherished. We didn't have much, but we had all we needed.

FAMILY

When 2009 rolled around and we decided to start a family, Sean took on a job at a large national insurance company. It was a company at which his dad had enjoyed a long career. I remember being on tour somewhere in Sweden (I toured for a time with Nina Persson from The Cardigans) when Sean called me to tell me he got the job. I was shopping when he phoned to tell me and I remember stopping cold in the middle of the store, somehow feeling like this was a significant moment. I couldn't say why. Maybe because it was a remarkably different endeavour for him.

Touring and singing while pregnant is quite a beast. At seven months, I played a show in Stratford, Ontario, opening up for The Guess Who's Randy Bachman at the Festival Theatre, which housed an iconic thrust stage where the audience could take in the show from three sides. Whether I was determined to continue my touring, or whether I was simply fuelled by my love for music, taking a break from music and singing just wasn't part of my plan. I was gonna keep goin'! To this day, many people remind me of that show, of how incredibly pregnant I was, strumming my guitar a bit awkwardly, playing my keyboard, and doing my thing. I was exhausted, but with a baby bouncing around inside me, flipping around at unexpected times and exploring the real estate of my uterus, I felt alive and exhilarated. Making music and carrying life. You couldn't have this experience and not be in awe of it.

After my son was born, I was euphoric. Although he was born prematurely at 34 weeks and five days, Ronan was born healthy. He gained weight quickly, despite my troubles nursing at first — and I found myself in heaven, cuddling him and watching his every move. As he slept, I wrote music. The midwives would come regularly to check on us and weigh him in a little sack. I was able to release *Gem and I*, my duets record that Greg Wells had partially produced and Frank had helped mix. I felt that I had it all — a family, a beautiful little son, a partner, a music career. I sang Ronan lullabies; I sang him to sleep. I rocked him endlessly. I strolled him for hours down sidewalk blocks, and I wrote him music. And two years later, my daughter came, and right there, we truly had the whole package. A little girl and a little boy, a beautiful old home, and as Sean worked his new job, I settled into my role as a stay-at-home mom, writing music in between it all.

FAST-FORWARD TO 2016

I was a complete and total wreck. My entire body shook as I stood alone in the middle of Springbank Park in London, Ontario. It's a strange feeling to shake uncontrollably in public, but as things had become so suffocating and impossible around me, other humans, their stories, the murmur of their conversations faded quickly into the periphery of neighbouring trees and chilly autumn air.

Sean had decided to leave our marriage and start a new life with a woman he had met at work, and the shock and pain of this revelation was immeasurable. I'll never forget the day he confirmed it, as we sat in his car after a parent-teacher meeting at the school. "Me and the kids will be waiting for you in the house," I told him, pushing the words out through tears, unable to catch a breath. He cried, too, in a display of the vulnerability we so desperately could have used during the past decade. I thought our ability to show ourselves this rawness had frozen long ago, but as everything was ending before my eyes, I saw the love and vulnerability, like a gold ring you thought you might have lost forever somehow floating to the surface of the ocean, only to sink back down again. No desperate swipe of a hand could recover it. Sean was gone.

At bedtime, which I now did alone, I tucked in my kids and openly wept in their beds. What should have been a happy story time saw me, broken and helpless, completely unaware of where to put these devastating feelings of abandonment except blathered out on the printed pillows of my children's beds.

What I'm leaving out of the story is the demise of our relationship, but it bears no importance on how grief-stricken and gutted I felt that fall of 2016. Whether it was a mutual lack of awareness or connection, a failure to honour and befriend one another, or just falling prey to the pressures of parenthood and responsibility, I won't detail it here. I will say that from my point of view, our problems seemed similar to those of many other couples who meet and fall in love in their twenties and have children. Despite what happened, I felt then and I feel now that when you create a family, your priority is to protect it, work for it because it's a precious choice made together consciously.

So I tried to fight for my family as I knew it. I begged for a chance to attend counselling, to right the wrongs, to really dive into who we were and who we'd become. I was ready to get vulnerable and make some positive change. My pleas were met with silence. All of the years, all of the joy and pain of birth and early motherhood, all of the wishes for growing old together with a friend, holding each other through family funerals, celebrating kids' milestones, were gone.

There were days that I tried to go for my morning run, but I couldn't even make it twenty feet around the block. I felt like a skeleton, a set of bones just held together by tiny bits of tissue, trying to move itself, crying out for normalcy but overcome by a weakness that felt terminal.

THE THEATRE

Now there's nothing quite like being left by your husband and being asked to be in a play where you have to sing dozens of Joni Mitchell songs, but that's what happened. Six days after the teary conversation in the car after parent-teacher interviews, I went into rehearsals for *Joni Mitchell: River* at the Grand Theatre. I had known for most of the summer that I'd be in the play, which was the brainchild of Allen MacInnis. Allen, who had already directed the play in Vancouver and Winnipeg, had crafted a love story to be told through the performance of 30 Joni songs. I was one of three actors who would sing them. Perfect, I remember thinking, sooooo many songs about love, loss, and the complex experience of being a woman. At one turn, I was furious at everything and everyone on the planet; at another, I was grateful to be asked to be in the play because I had always loved theatre but never been given the chance to perform. Still, I was in survival mode. I knew my kids needed their meals, their mom, and some semblance of contentment in the house. I asked my own mom for help.

I had gone to the doctor to find a way to cope, simply to make it through a day. I was in shock, and I wasn't sleeping. If I didn't sleep, I knew I couldn't perform or sing, and as much as my life was in tatters, I didn't want to let down the cast and crew of the play: Brandon Wall, a charming actor from Toronto; assistant director Thom Allison, who had rocked Sondheim plays and a cult sci-fi TV series called *Killjoys*; and, most notably, Louise Pitre. A Dora Award winner and a Tony Award nominee for her work in *Mamma Mia* on Broadway, Louise was a legend. As I entered rehearsals, I became keenly aware that I was not the focal point. No one was asking about my music or time with David Bowie. Every conversation was about theatre, Joni's work, and preparing for the play. In a way, this was a gift because it meant no one knew much about me, and for a few minutes out of the day, when I focused on the songs, I forgot my pain.

When I left the theatre, I could see Sean's workplace — the shiny high-rise building, One London Place, towering over me in the blinding sunshine. Often, across the street at St. Peter's Cathedral, midday bells would unapologetically chime, and a bride and groom would spill out of the church surrounded by laughter, friends, and family. These sights were like a knife in my heart, and as I'd go walk the neighbourhood to get lunch, it felt like my blood and guts were spilling all over the road and everyone was pointing and laughing. In the ultimate assault, like something from a bad movie, I walked down Clarence Street one day on a lunch break, and I saw him and her, laughing and walking to his car from their office. I don't remember anything that happened in the 15 minutes after that moment, as I tucked into a hair salon and pretended to be interested in the bottles on the shelf. My heart was beating a zillion miles a minute, and my breath seemed gone. All

I could think when I finally regained some consciousness was, That's *my* Sean.

Deliriousness and desperation set in. I lost ten pounds. For someone with my small frame and height of five-foot-two, a weight loss of ten pounds felt significant. I tried to seem like I had my life together, booking last-minute into Chatters, a hair salon in London, to go all blond and then shopping for the sexiest push-up bras I could find. I was in no state of mind for this makeover, but I went for it anyway. Everyone with a head on their shoulders knows that true beauty comes from within, but during those months I felt ugly inside and out. Old and ugly. Thrown out. So I was gonna do something about it. At the strip mall.

People started to find out about my breakup, and to have to tell them what was going on was terrible for me. I began drinking regularly and, as I noted earlier in the book, smoking. Sometimes, because Sean had left a great deal of his belongings in the house, I'd light up, crank the music as loud as I could in the car, and in a more polite version of "dumping stuff on the front lawn," I'd load everything of his that I could carry into a storage unit at the edge of town. As vilified and betrayed as I felt, I still put his items in the unit carefully. Because, well, I still loved him.

Delusion, confusion, and madness whipped around me like a tornado filled with blunt objects. It felt like suffering blow after blow after humiliating blow.

———

There came a point that I now consider my lowest. I started to feel sick and feared that I might have a bladder infection. On bad days, I wondered if I might have a more serious illness related to my reproductive organs. I couldn't figure out why I was having so much discharge out of my body, a discoloured liquid that I had never seen before. I finally went to the doctor, and they decided to do a pelvic exam. And let me tell you, when you're left alone with two little kids, without the support of a partner, and your only lifeline is a bottle of anti-anxiety meds in your medicine cabinet, spread-legged on a hospital table is the last place you want to be. But in another sense, I already felt ripped bare of everything anyway, so it didn't matter. The nurse poked around, I squirmed, and eventually, she informed me that I had a tampon lodged inside. I couldn't believe it. It had been there for quite some time, and I guess I had just been too overwhelmed to remember to take it out or even know it was there. The nurse, someone I would have to see again and again in town because my community is so small, left the room and returned with some tool to get it out. Once she'd disposed of the tampon and left the room, I cried endlessly. I can't even take care of myself, I thought. I left feeling humiliated, trying to forget the indignant, intolerable smell of the appointment, and walked back into a life I can only describe as dark and impossible.

JONI

In the midst of all the pain, there was the theatre. I couldn't say no to the chance to sing on this stage. Well, I could have bowed out, but I didn't want to. The distraction was welcome — something different in a landscape of hurt, and something fresh in a life filled with so much domestic responsibility.

I loved Joni Mitchell's *Blue* record. The bravery in her lyrics, the exploration of self and love, the stream-of-consciousness playfulness of "All I Want" and the torturous lull of "Blue" were part of my DNA. Now, so many more of her songs would be part of my life for six weeks straight as I dove into performing in *River*.

Allen assigned a cross-section of songs just for me: "River," "Hejira," "Carey," "Dog Eat Dog," "The Magdalene Laundries," and "Coyote," among others. As an ensemble we would share the duties on "Free Man in Paris," "Big Yellow Taxi," and "Both Sides Now." This was not a biographical play, nor was it a concert. *River* was a telling of a story through music. I'm not sure many people understood this play's format — which contained no spoken dialogue, just singing — but all the same, I was determined to be great and sing Joni with all my heart. All of London and the area were going to see me, and though I was cracked inside, I considered this my theatre debut. I don't count a brief stint when I was 11 years old and played a potato-sack-wearing orphan with no lines in *Annie* at a rural playhouse.

Preparation for this role was three-tiered. I felt I needed:

1. vocal maintenance and check in,
2. to find some way to feel confident, and
3. to know the material inside and out.

The obstacles to success were:

1. fatigue and stress,
2. feelings of inadequacy, and
3. nervousness fuelled by lack of experience and having little time to prepare.

Despite knowing what had to be done to crush this role, and despite my track record as a singer, I still felt unsure that I would survive this play. I knew there was a very big chance that I could be an embarrassment.

Although the distraction of being at the Grand Theatre was good for me, every night after rehearsal I'd return to a house that wasn't the home I'd imagined. My emails to my husband were nothing short of manic and scattered. I titled one *Begging you* and began it with *I go through every minute of the day nauseous, anxious, and fighting to keep my head up.* These messages went unanswered.

The obstacles to my success multiplied as rehearsal days went on.

Although Joni had performed the bulk of her songs with a sweet tone and folk twang, the director wanted me to belt songs liked "Carey" and "Big Yellow Taxi." At first, I quietly balked at this idea, but then I realized that this wasn't a coffee house, this was theatre. Allen was experienced, and he was also an intuitive, gentle soul, and I trusted him. I was mostly daunted by the hugely important task of performing "River," an iconic, well-loved song that I dreaded screwing up by feeling nervous or frail. I knew that I would have to rise to the occasion, hold those notes that sustained like a long sunset, and capture the melancholic, Christmassy vibe of the song. And this song, with lyrics that were all-too-familiar, occurred in the play near its end, when the story moves towards its all-important resolution. How will I ever get through this song? How will I ever belt the word "fly" that is so high and holds so long when I can barely breathe? I wondered through a steady stream of tears. My life had become the song "River." I wanted that river — needed that river — to skate away on and never come back.

Knowing vocal preparation would be essential for me, I went back to Mitch. I was extremely sad in his company, but I was determined, if not to succeed in the play, to be good for my kids again. Mitch, who also had young kids, could relate. He was warm and sensitive, and his studio was a safe place where I had been able to be myself since age 19. Seeing Mitch was emotional, not just because of what I was going through, but because his presence was a reminder of how much of my life had passed and how many people I had been throughout my career, how many sacrifices I had made, some worthwhile and some not.

I sang through "River" in front of Mitch. He plunked out the notes of the melody on the keyboard to see where they were and reminded me that I had sung those notes and many much higher without difficulty before. "It's not that high," he said to me in a way that implied *You can do this*. I realized that my feelings of inadequacy and the challenges in my voice at that time were really rooted in stress.

The play did not involve dancing, but it did involve choreographed moves. In "Help Me," we had very specific places to move across the stage, up and down. We, the actors, interacted with each other as we sang, and I'll admit it was this part of the play that felt foreign to me and posed a massive challenge. A dancer I am not, and, what's more, to move in front of other humans while singing has never been my strong suit. Just as mimicking Beck and covering my stage in caution tape was the wrong choice, so were the times I pranced across the stage in the middle of pop songs during 2002 when I wasn't sure who the heck I was. In my rock band, I seem to know how to move, guided purposefully by the music and the loud crack of drums and guitars. But in the Joni play? I was a fish out of water.

As I moved around the rehearsal stage in front of Allen and Thom, I could see a look of absolute fear come together on their faces. I was tanking. I was stiff, I was self-conscious. I was like a dachshund who had just come out of a coma and had been asked to dance with the grace of Fred Astaire.

And then there was Louise. A vibrant, accomplished grand dame of the stage, who spent her time working out in the morning and smoking cigarettes unapologetically at night. She knew everyone and everything, a sort of glamorous anarchist. She was a sight to behold, and an inspiration to be near. Her partner Joe was younger, a handsome actor who'd sometimes come to town just to be with her. They were so in love, and she was so thrilling to be around. The other thing about her was her kindness. She was gentle with the pop star who had joined the cast. She made conversation with me even though I sensed she wanted to be somewhere else some of the time. I drew from the strength of her powerful energy, and she pushed me to get over myself.

This would be the first of many reminders of the unique

power of being near other women. And during this time, I was carefully held by my girlfriends. Whether it was a word by text, a hug, a tear, I knew that the friendships I had and have with women were sustaining. They were healing. My girlfriends seemed to understand and listen in a way that no one else could. My own mother, Linda, was also one of my greatest friends and helped so graciously during this time. Although I didn't tell Louise about my breakup, I did tell Greg Lowe, the musical director, and Allen. On a break, I mustered up the courage to announce to them that I was sorry if I seemed off here and there. "I'm going through a separation." I said, and, with my self-worth still in the toilet, assured them both that it wouldn't affect the play. They took the information in without asking many questions, and we all went our separate ways for a lunch break. It wasn't as though they didn't care, but perhaps they weren't expecting my news or didn't know what to do with it. I felt like Allen immediately knew, although he didn't say it at the time, that singing would actually prove to be a gift for me.

DO OR DIE

Still, I felt out of place and like I was flirting with failure. Rehearsals continued to truck along, and I was still stiff and awkward. Every day, opening night got closer. The real deal. Actual humans in seats. Paying humans. Journalists. The artistic director of the theatre looking on.

Paralyzed by fear, I decided about two weeks into rehearsal to go to the apartment I was staying at in London and do the last thing I wanted to do. I turned the camera phone on my frail, 105-pound body. I saw a woman who was broken, unloved, unattractive, and confused. Still, I decided to hit record on my phone and sing my songs along with the choreographed moves. This felt absolutely frightening and ridiculous, but I followed through, and, most importantly, I watched myself back.

———

In the mid 1990s, I went out to a small bar in Berkeley, California. My brother had been doing some work with a band playing there, and he got both of us in for free. I loved being somewhere as beautiful as California, out with my brother and seeing musicians do their thing in a brand new place. I noticed that after their first set, the whole band retired to the dressing room and listened to a recording of what they had just played in the club. I found this extremely bizarre. What? I thought to myself. They're not back there drinking Bud Light and eating pita chips? I couldn't believe they'd choose to listen to everything they just played! That band was Train, and they went on to sell over ten million albums.

Having the balls to look at yourself, and hear yourself back, this was a lesson that I learned from them, and I put into action my own version of it that fateful fall. **Secret No. 23: Watch and listen to yourself.**

———

When I watched myself on video and heard myself sing, I could see expressions on my face that didn't suit the song.

I could see the stiffness in my jaw. I could see the rigidity in my movements. This was stress that, like some kind of ancient physical restraint put on me against my will, had taken full, unrelenting hold of my body. The stress of losing my partner and my life. The stress of fear itself. I was afraid to fail. I was afraid to be myself, because being myself had so far not worked out well for me. I was afraid of ruining the play. I was afraid of this huge theatre laughing at Emm Gryner, the pop star, freshly dumped, trying to be a theatre actor. I was afraid that Joni Mitchell's immensely intricate songwriting, vocal stylings, and energy would be butchered by a girl who had no business singing in the first place. I was sucked right back into chicken world, to a place where singing was discouraged at the dinner table, hymns were mumbled through, and I grasped at anything I could to be seen and heard, to feel love and be loved in a way beyond my accomplishments.

I broke down in tears during this filming. Yet, I videoed myself again. And again. Until my voice sounded like it should have. Until my choreographed moves looked like I had some semblance of confidence. Did I actually have confidence? Probably not, but I could trick myself and others into thinking I had it together. Just the same way that during my first rehearsal with David, I did not have it together, either, yet I made a commitment the next day to be great.

When I went back into rehearsals and performed the songs, a huge change occurred. For the first time, I knew how I looked and sounded to the cast and directors. I did the work of gathering more information. As I sang and moved, Allen and Thom's faces beamed for the first time! The cast seemed to relax. Finally, I decided, this play had a chance. I had a chance.

SURVIVAL TACTICS

One upside of working at an established theatre was that they had provided each member of the cast with a free gym membership at a fitness club downtown. In order to combat the feelings of weakness, I made use of it. Road running was no longer working out for me, but there was something about going to the gym that offered a little more comfort. I could start small. I was surrounded by walls, other people, staff. There was a water fountain nearby the equipment. I could set the treadmill speed low. I could get my limbs moving. I worked my way up from small runs to 20-minute runs. Increasing my breathing capacity was key for singing through this time. Even just being on the treadmill for the length of four or five songs helped me so much. And getting started was, as everyone says, the hard part. Once I had begun, I had given myself a gift. On days when I woke up anxious or feeling tired, I went to the gym. Brandon did this as well. We both used that opportunity to move ourselves into a realm of feeling prepared for the stage. And Louise, well . . . being the consummate pro she was, Louise was going all the time already, doing a combo of weights and cardio, and sometimes going with Joe.

My habits behind the scenes were not great. I wasn't drinking during performances or rehearsals, but I was smoking. I couldn't break this habit, and I'll admit I did the play, and many other musical things for a while afterwards, as a smoker. It was only after I quit (a year and a half later) that I noticed a massive change in the capacity of my breath, my overall health, and my ability to sustain notes. I wish that I had gone through the play without smoking, but when you're trying to survive it's hard to align your actions with your values. By no means do I suggest that it's okay to take up a bunch of bad habits to get through something difficult, but the underlying feelings of inadequacy, victimization, and frustration that come up as the result of life's curveballs are all normal. In fact, part of singing or doing anything through the dark times in our lives is to allow ourselves to feel as shitty as we need to and take hold of whatever we need to survive and move through the pain. When trauma arises, sometimes we need to surrender before we are ready for powerful remedies. Remedies are hard to find in the dark. Sometimes we need to be in the dark for a long time before our eyes adjust.

When my eyes finally adjusted, I realized that every time I had a cigarette, even just one once in a while, I was "a smoker." Emm Gryner is not a smoker, I knew deep inside. I also started to realize that smoking wasn't a reward. With every smoke break, I was feeding an addiction. I downloaded the app Smoke Free, I vaped an e-cigarette to wean myself off nicotine, I employed some old-fashioned will-power, and I got my values clear in focus. I noticed that a lot of the people I knew who smoked had a host of other bad habits, too, so I kept that in mind. I distanced myself, as best I could, from others who smoked or would encourage me. Sticking to my vision for health and wanting to be the best me for my kids and the best singer I could be, I was able to finally quit two years after my break-up. But you quit when you're ready; and during the play, I wasn't ready.

LITTLE VICTORIES

Opening night finally came and nerves set in. I drew strength from the people around me. I relied on my breath. I accepted that it might not be perfect and there may be some mistakes. I trusted that I had done the work.

The night was a success. I was nervous through some songs, but I shined. The whole run went swimmingly. At the beginning of it, I began singing "River" with tears welling up at the edges of my eyes, but I ended the three-week run by singing it with confidence and sometimes without even a thought about my marriage. My then-mother-in-law came to the play twice. She knew everything I was feeling. I sang through regardless. Some nights I laughed in the wings. Some nights I felt exhausted. The cast and crew bonded, and the house was packed every night.

As is often the case, closing night was bittersweet. I knew that real life loomed. I would be walking off the theatre stage and back into a life of being at home with the kids every day, without a partner and without the distraction of the theatre. Still, I couldn't help but feel like a survivor. I had let singing save me.

Much later — maybe two years later — at a concert I did at a local opry, I ran into a stranger who had seen *Joni Mitchell: River*. "You were amazing in that play," she told me as she dished some food from the buffet onto her plate before the music started. "You and the guitar player were my favourite part!" she said. I smiled, knowing what it had taken to get through it. I smiled, feeling like everything I had experienced in those hard days was almost ancient history.

Faced with the task of singing through difficult times, the following ways in which I attended to my needs made it bearable and even at times enjoyable:

1. **I took it one day at a time.** No, one hour at a time. No, one minute at a time.
2. **I asked for help.** (There, I've said it again.) I asked for help from my doctor, my vocal coach, and my mom. You may not have three or two or even one person readily available to help you in a crisis, but you must look far enough to find someone to talk to. The stigma on the struggle with mental health is lifting, and there exist organizations, hotlines, websites, chat lines, online therapy, 12-step programs, community programs — you name it — where you can find help if you feel you have absolutely no one.

   No one is above asking for help. Counsellors have counsellors. Doctors have doctors. My doctor gave me anti-anxiety meds to help me sleep through the night, and this made it possible for me to cope during the day. I was careful not to become addicted to these meds, and I was happy to eventually wean myself off them.

I was the last person I ever thought would need something like that, yet they were part of my healing.

I asked for help from Mitch, who showed me what I needed to do to sing through what I felt were difficult pieces. He reminded me of my strength and my years of experience.

I asked my family for help — my mom and my brothers got me through, whether it was lending a hand or listening to me cry.

3. **I allowed myself to feel pain.** I allowed the pain to visit. Well, no, I allowed the pain to flipping move in, unpack twelve suitcases, and start using my toothbrush. My favourite quote by Ijeoma Umebinyuo is at the top of this chapter: "Allow the pain to visit . . ."

4. **I made steps towards physical fitness.** They may have been small steps, but I made them. And don't forget, singing, even at the worst of times, is still a sport, and you may feel injured inside and out, but very small steps toward increasing breath capacity can help your healing process.

5. **I surrounded myself with others.** I don't think I could have shone the way I needed to had I been touring my own concerts. Those concerts see me in charge of every detail, from selecting the band to figuring out what we're eating before each show. This play demanded that I just show up and do the work. This play had other people

involved and money riding on it. This play — to me — needed to be great to make the entire production great. My desire to not let down the audience, the cast, and ultimately myself, pushed me to draw my voice out of its dungeon and to sing Joni's songs with heart. I pushed myself to let my voice expand across a beautiful historic stage, largely because others were involved.

6. **I told myself I can do it**, even if I felt very easily, at any moment, I could be totally useless. Just telling myself I could do it allowed some part of me to believe it was possible.

7. **I accepted that every song, every moment, and every night of this play might not be perfect.** And that's okay.

8. My children. **I knew I had to do better for my family.** They deserved a mom who could rise above. In a world where we are so often in charge of our children, this was a case where they spoke to me, whether they knew it or not. They sent me the message that I needed to and could do better.

ACTION ITEMS

1. **Make a list of two to three people you can ask for help from in times of distress.** There's no one on the face of the planet who can do everything alone.

2. **Surround yourself with other humans** in times of darkness, even if you don't feel like it at first.

3. **Allow yourself a musical break.** If this means no singing for a while, this means no singing. Sometimes the breaks are necessary, and you just might come back recharged.
4. **Accept your voice.** Accept that it won't be perfect, and that's okay.
5. Take tiny steps towards some physical activity. **Move your body**, even the tiniest bit, and you'll start coming out of the dark.
6. **Remember what matters to you.**

CHAPTER 19

DEVELOPING A SOLID TONE

"I saw sorrow turning into clarity."
— YOKO ONO

In Chapter 12, you read about "line and movement" and focusing the sound. As a novice singer, this was one of the aspects of singing that led to my ability to become powerful onstage and on record. Without focusing my sound and gaining this solid tone, I would not have been able to sing clearly at arenas, sing big pop choruses, or endure the most difficult time in my life while singing and moving around onstage. I also noticed a connection between mind and body here — being direct with my voice led to increased confidence in my life, and therefore I became more clear and direct in my decision-making and my outlook on life.

Secret No. 24: Sing with a solid tone.

What the heck does this even mean? The concept of *solid tone* can be difficult to wrap your head around, but the good news is that it is 50 percent mental and 50 percent physical.

That means that even if executing the exercises is challenging, you can be working on the mental part of it which requires little to no understanding of your instrument.

As a young girl, my voice was "breathy." Many singers who are untrained have a breathy voice, which can feel unfocused, wavering, and, at times, unsteady. Despite the rawness of my voice, I liked the breathiness of my singing sound. It soothed me. Unfortunately, I couldn't carry on singing that way, because I had no power, no versatility, and no strength. Also, singing that way for too long would have injured me because I was relying on the throat and upper lungs to create the sound. Eventually, the work that I did to strengthen my diaphragmatic muscle was the gateway for moving into working on solid tone. Think of it like a pizza. Belly breathing connected with the source of power was the dough upon which I could pile everything else. But if you haven't worked on belly breathing, you're just piling pizza sauce and toppings on thin air. So once you have begun to combine diaphragmatic breathing with the source of power, you can start to really focus on getting a solid tone and suddenly you have a jumbo pizza with perfect dough and all the toppings you like.

When we have a weak or untrained voice, we accept that those things are part of our voice. We tell ourselves that this is what we are working with, and we've been working with this our whole lives. This is somewhat true, but in actual fact, when you think this way you are just looking at the flour in the pizza dough, gazing at it. Nothing's getting made. You're just . . . flour-gazing? Uh-huh. That tone that you are so used to is actually only a particle of powder in a much greater, richer, stronger recipe. What's more, we're sometimes attached to the negative qualities we have settled for in our voice. When we begin to open the door to growth, to new exercises, to hearing our voice in any new way, we can feel a sense of excitement, but we can also feel panic. This is fear of the unknown. It's easier to take a road you've travelled a hundred times than to go off and find some mysterious backroads. Who knows how long taking those backroads will delay you? What if you get lost? What if the roads are unpaved? What if there are detours? Coyotes? What if there are no gas stations?

Many singers become afraid that they will lose the things they love about their natural, untrained voice. They worry they will sound completely different and don't even want to bother with trying on new ways of working. But take it from me: it's important to get over this fear.

Developing a strong, solid tone is actually the ultimate way to nurture that natural voice. By seeing your voice as moving in a "line" ("line and movement"), you strengthen it, you don't change it. Many of the exercises I'm talking about right now will only temporarily change the way your voice sounds. But slowly, over time, you will experience your new, powerful voice as one that has everything — the timbre and flavours you always loved, but also a strength and richness.

Many things in life that involve great change are often the result of upheaval. There is a stepping into the unknown, and it's in this adventure where change can occur.

MENTAL

Let's begin with the mental part of "line and movement." Often when we think of our range or our register, we think of a piano keyboard: its expansive 88-key wilderness, those rumbling low notes and those ridiculously high plinky notes. Or we think of our voice in the context of many choir voices, or the sizable palette of an orchestra. It's wonderful to know that we have the ability in our body to make a wide range of note choices, but to the new singer, this can be scary. Going into the heavens of falsetto or head voice can feel frightening or tight, or it can bring on feelings of inadequacy. Going into the low register can sound like we are characters in a horror film, our voices pitched down a few hundred octaves. The idea of using the mind to step out of this fear of overwhelm when it comes to register can be exciting. **Instead of viewing the voice as a mountain range of very high peaks and very low ravines, see the voice as a forward moving stream of sound, or a river with the sound outside the body.**

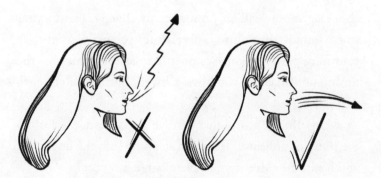

Given how I see the voice, it is odd then that "River" was such a monumental and difficult song for me to tackle in the Joni Mitchell play. Every night, sometimes twice a day, I sang "I wish I had a river." And oddly enough, I did. I had the river of my voice. And it would be that vision, that sense of sound coming out purposefully that would carry me out of darkness, if only for a moment.

A river flows out and forward, and while it may meet some degree of varying elevation, it is still, usually, a river flowing forward in its natural state. To really focus on this idea of your sound flowing out and forward, to the back of a hall or venue, or out into the sky of an open-air stadium, I want you to envision your voice like that beautiful, strong river moving ever forward. Think of a steady plane that is natural, forward, direct, and purposeful. And just as a river replenishes the earth and delivers goodness to organisms, animals, plants, and humans, so does the voice deliver possibility, expression, joy, and purpose.

Some singers I've worked with have come up with their own visualizations for "line and movement" in sound. One singer I worked with named Tracie saw her sound coming out like the movement of a trombone. Logan, another singer with whom I work, freely uses her hands to mimic the flow of sound coming forward. Find whatever vision works for you, and begin to see your voice moving that way. Not up and down, but forward and even slightly down. This doesn't mean you limit your voice or flatten it, this means you focus it. And all of the notes — high and low — can exist in this more focused place outside of the body.

PHYSICAL

The physical part of focusing your sound takes time. A very simple equation will help you understand where developing a solid tone fits into your practice:

BELLY BREATHING
SOURCE OF POWER
+ LINE AND MOVEMENT
———————————————
STRONG VOICE

Focusing the sound won't be the first thing you do. The first step really is to start using the source of power that is your diaphragm and your intercostal muscles instead of your higher chest and your upper lungs.

Focus your sound so that any extraneous air is not escaping from the edges of your mouth, and the sound is not coming through your nasal cavity. It's almost like the sound has found an imaginary tunnel or a sweet spot. This requires a relaxation of the jaw, the chin, and the face to correctly achieve. Visit my website and watch my video on developing a solid tone to help you visualize and experience this technique with a little more clarity. The sound that you make when you focus may be almost unpretty. This is not the beautiful, airy sound that you use to sing "Careless Whisper" on a summer drive through the countryside. This is the sound of the tip of a ballpoint pen, not a two-inch wide paint brush. You are using your source of power to make a clear, strong sound. It is the difference between delivering welcoming remarks at a convention and the whisper of a lullaby. It is, at first, commanding and direct.

———

The popular misconception in both finding the source of power and homing in on a focused sound is that the singer needs to push. You don't need to push, you need to soften and use what comes naturally. Again, we are rediscovering what worked for us as babies. When babies cry or yell, they do not sound like The Weeknd. There is nothing smooth about the noise they make. But they are also not pushing. A baby doesn't scream for 20 minutes and then sound like she has lost her voice. Maybe, if you're trapped with one on an airplane, you'd wish that baby would lose their voice! But babies don't lose their voices because they are using the diaphragm naturally, just as it was meant to be used, and the vocal cords are simply vibrating and doing their normal work.

Also, the more you rely on your source of power, the easier it is to find the solid tone. There should be no pushing, no strain, no veins popping out on your neck (check your mirror or video yourself for this). The bulk of the movement and sound comes from below. And in all cases, relax the upper body, the shoulders, the jaw, the neck, chin, and tongue. This is another piece of great news for people who are working so hard to elevate their voice. **Relaxation is one of the best routes to success in this part of the development of your voice.**

Check out my video at emmgryner.com/videos for more clarity on this part of your practice.

Eventually, you will find a directness of tone in your voice, a richness — and if you follow the steps for good vocal health and move through your work with a sense of acceptance and non-judgment, you will find clarity in your day-to-day as well.

ACTION ITEMS

1. **Approach finding a solid tone with relaxation.** Stretch your facial muscles, do some neck and shoulder yoga, explore meditation with an eye to relaxing and feeling confident in your voice. On your exhale, consciously relax parts of your body, especially shoulders and jaw.

2. **Really make sure you understand the source of power for your singing.** Do not attempt to find a solid tone unless you feel you can make some sound with belly breathing. If you still are unsure on this, video yourself doing warm-ups or singing, and see if you are activating that all-important lower body. If you see your chest and upper lungs rise consistently, it's a sign that you're not doing it quite right yet.

3. **Visualize your sound as coming "out and down," "forward and purposeful."** If you are practising online with a teacher or doing videos, sing over and beyond your laptop screen and pick a point far in the distance to sing to. Our sound can reach further than we think.

4. **Watch my video on solid tone.** Accept for a while that the sound will be unlike what you are used to, and not necessarily very pretty. That's because you are building a voice that has strength; later you can dial back in all of the nuance and flavour that you love about your existing voice.

CHAPTER 20

RETURNING TO YOUR TRUE SELF

"Always be a first rate version of yourself and
not a second rate version of someone else."
— JUDY GARLAND

After finishing the Joni play, I was thrust back into real life. There was no extra help to cushion me as I walked back into the role of full-time mom. There were endless mysteries to navigate, and no one with whom to navigate them — but at the end of the day, I needed to show up for my kids. Bad habits continued to swirl around me. I recklessly dove into dating, something I was nowhere near ready to do. But it wasn't all terrible. Some good time was spent when I poured my heart into an ambient album, which showcased layers and layers of my softest voice. It was a project I could work on while my children slept, and it was the one thing that I did just three months after my marriage imploded that was a small step towards healing. And surprise, it featured my voice. Heavily.

The album was called *Aonarán* (pronounced AY-nu-ron), which is Gaelic for "solitary person." I wrote lyrics that were more felt than heard, and my voice stretched across the Pro Tools screen in long, smooth waveforms. Sometimes I'd ask Frank, who was mixing it, to reverse the soundwaves; sometimes I'd want him to just mask the poetry in heaps of reverb and delay. While many of my peers thought I had every right to make a death metal album, I was, once again, inspired by my son and daughter. I thought to myself what I would want them to have if they had to go through this, or anything else of such immense difficulty. I'd want them to have encouraging words, wrapped up in optimistic but gentle soundwaves. In the past, my music always needed to "say something," but on these songs, I needed the work to be the sonic equivalent of a warm embrace. That was what *Aonarán* was. Without my knowing it, my voice was starting to wrap around me and begin the healing process even though my mind and body were miles away from being healthy.

But I needed more.

GREG

As I looked towards the next pop album, I welcomed collaboration in a way I never had before. I planned to record *Only of Earth: Days of Games*, the first in a trilogy of albums inspired by a sci-fi story that I had dreamed up over the past years. I had been so inspired by the musical director on the Joni play, Greg Lowe. He was a slim, grey-haired rock 'n' roller and jazz guitarist in his fifties from Winnipeg, who brought his gentle, confident spirit to rehearsals and the set. Fiercely bonded with his partner, Josephine, since 1979, he embodied all I felt I could never have. He lived a life of love, purpose, and music and did it all with wisdom and freedom of spirit.

I invited Greg to play guitar on *Only of Earth* as I loved his soloing so much. His playing on the Joni play and on his own records was warm, intricate, and reckless but had tonalities of jazz and bebop. I even went to lengths to create music for the album with long solo sections that he could fill. I wrote a song called "The Spark," which tapped into Black Sabbath roots, something I knew Greg had fallen in love with when he was around ten years old. This was the first album I made as a solo artist that didn't see me asking musicians to layer themselves over my songs. The musicians on *Only of Earth* really made the songs. My drummer friend Tim Timleck shaped the '70s and '80s rock feel of the album considerably with his impeccable feel and power. I built upon his drum parts because they were so musical — and being musical isn't something that all drummers are known to be. Opening myself up to collaborating with others was another form of healing. It influenced how strong and diverse my vocal takes were on *Only of Earth* and, even though I was too blind to see it, a stronger voice was starting to emerge.

Greg's presence on my record was significant to my healing process, but so was knowing him. During some downtime during the run of the play, Greg and a few other cast members went out to see Earth, Wind & Fire and Chicago play at an arena. As we sat in the third-row seats that I had scored us, we drank and laughed, and I tried to forget my troubles for one night. Greg sat next to me, and as I sipped my whiskey I told him more about my separation.

Intrigued by his calm and in awe of his long relationship with Jo, I asked him what the secret was. What Greg said to me changed my life forever. He paused for a moment and then said to me, "Emm, everyone wants something. We all want, want, want. But when it comes to a relationship, you have to ask yourself, 'What can I offer?'"

Tears filled my eyes as the members of Earth, Wind & Fire filed onstage one after another. A simple answer, a simple concept. *What can I offer?* This had eluded me for the 16 years I'd been with my husband. Where else had I forgotten this in life? As the show began and the crowd roared, I dried the tears and breathed deeply, feeling like I had just discovered treasure. The voices onstage swept us all away for the night, something we all needed.

In April of 2017, as I was working on *Only of Earth*, I still felt very much like a victim, and I was managing horribly, having bouts of anger that stemmed from this feeling of being left without a say in the most important relationships of my life. On the other hand, I felt some joy in working on a new album. Doing something creative provided a small escape from the fact that life was crumbling all around me. Greg's involvement was a great distraction — the solos he was sending were amazing, and the acoustic guitars and electrics he layered onto my songs from his studio in Winnipeg were world-class. So you can imagine my surprise and shock, when one day he wrote to me, "I have to make the next song the last. I have some things in my life that need my TLC."

I was beyond disappointed. In a smaller way, I felt like a victim again, abandoned and stuck with bad news. I couldn't understand why he would jump ship in the middle of a record. The recording was all going so well, and I'd be hard-pressed to find another guitar player to match his sound. I shoved my ego aside and thanked him for his work. One month later, Allen wrote to me to tell me Greg Lowe had passed away. As I read the email in my kitchen, I dropped my phone onto the counter. I sobbed. He had had liver cancer, had battled it all through the play, and had obviously been living with the final stages of it while playing on my songs. This moment shaped me forever — the devastation, the shock, and the loss. This, Greg playing on my music right up until the end, knowing he'd never hear it or see a penny from it, was the most beautiful display of that simple phrase, what can I offer?

This was the beginning of the return to my true self.

GLASTONBURY

A few years later, it was announced that the once-in-a-lifetime concert event I performed with Bowie, at Glastonbury Festival, would be available on video, vinyl, and CD for all to experience. The concert was considered one of the high points of Bowie's later career, a celebration of his life and legacy, where his greatest hits from "Starman" to "Ziggy Stardust," "Life on Mars?" to "Let's Dance" were aired to a hundred thousand adoring fans on an almost perfect night in June 2000 at Somerset Farm in England. Bowie had not performed at Glastonbury since 1971, so to return was thrilling for him. I remember him wearing a chic suit designed by Alexander McQueen, and I recalled Bowie's energy beaming off the stage to the farthest rows of the crowd and to all of us onstage.

When it was announced *Glastonbury 2000* would be released in 2018, I was intrigued, and I suppose pretty chuffed that something I sang on with David would be coming out to the world all these years later. Various media outlets approached me to talk about my time with Bowie and particularly my experience of singing at that concert. Although singing with David had been a wonderful part of my coming-of-age, it certainly seemed by then like it had happened a few million lifetimes ago. So many of my experiences with him — jet-setting and drinking champagne at 35,000 feet in first class (me, not him, he was not drinking by then), running around luxury hotels, and meeting up with other famous musicians all over the globe — eclipsed some of the actual craft of the experience.

I knew there were videos online which showed me singing with him, but over the course of almost two decades, I never really watched any of them. When *Glastonbury 2000* was announced and the media wanted to speak to me, I'll be honest, I panicked a little. How could I talk about something I didn't totally remember? Not to mention, I was still in so much emotional pain and my past accolades were shoved away like old photos in a shoebox in an attic.

One thing I've learned in my career is that when newspapers, magazines, and radio want to talk to you about something, you sure as hell better know what you're talking about or you'll be quoted saying the most idiotic things. I knew I'd have to do my homework and watch the concert back.

A friend of mine had found the concert online and sent it to me. You'd think a record company would make sure people in the video would actually get the video, but none of us did and I wasn't surprised. Big companies aren't known to think of the meaningful things. The day I decided to watch the concert, my mom was visiting me. For some reason, I said, in the same belaboured tone as someone who was about to be ushered in for a root canal, "Mom, I have to talk to people about this, so let's sit down and watch it."

Mom, always willing to watch anything I'm featured in, cheerily agreed, and I chefed up a couple of borderline car-cinogenic BLTs, threw them on some plates, and we fired up the laptop at my dining room table for a lunchtime screening of Glasto 2000.

Before we watched, I reflected on my feelings about David being gone. In some ways, two years on, his death was still haunting me, and I missed the sweet little private moments we shared. Processing his death from a place of ambiguity — neither a friend nor a stranger — was still hard for me. I couldn't turn to anyone in his close circle (I didn't even have their numbers anymore), and I knew that people around me who hadn't met him would not com-pletely understand the more intimate things I experienced while I toured with him: his demeanor, the way he was in rehearsal, the generous way he spent his time with us back-stage. Struggling with this and my feelings around Greg's passing, I put my own mortality under the microscope. Throw in the devastation of my marriage ending and it's safe to say that this lunchtime screening with my mom at my side was underscored by a wave of grief, despair, and loneliness that many of my former achievements could not eclipse with their wonderment.

We hit play.

Onscreen, my 25-year-old self walked onstage in big platform boots and spiky hair. I don't know who thought it was a good idea for me to slap a big fake tattoo of some snakes on my arm, but there it was, shining in the camera lights for all of Britain to see.

A few weeks before Glasto, David had lost his voice at some warm-up concerts we had done at Roseland Ballroom in New York, and as a result, we had to cancel some dates. As I watched the concert, it came back to me that the band and I went into Glastonbury slightly apprehensive and protective of DB (as we sometimes called him). You can see it in us if you watch the concert — we are all kind of "seeing how it goes" in the first few songs. David, no doubt infused by the energy of the crowd and the grandeur of the event, beamed his signature smile at the crowd, warmed up, and continued to amp up his performance minute by minute. Taking cues from our charming bandleader, we, too, loosened up. Our movements became more fluid. Eventually, I could see smiles exchanged across the stage. I remembered making those smiles. Sharing the stage with me were the cigarette-smoking rock guitar legend Earl Slick and Mike Garson. Gail Ann Dorsey was there, rocking the bass and belting out Freddie Mercury's famous part on "Under Pressure" with complete ease. Sterling Campbell, who knew Bowie's songs inside and out, was on the kit, and producer Mark Plati filled out the band with his lush twelve-string on songs like "Man Who Sold the World." The audience reaction was incredible, like nothing I had ever experienced. The sight of people went on for an eternity, they sang along — big blissful choruses. Music connected everyone as only music can. Melody wafted over the world.

As I watched the video next to my mom, I remembered things not shown on the screen — the body heat coming up out of the front rows, and at one point, seeing a crowd member being carried away by paramedics. The concerned Canadian in me watched from stage that night, wondering, Is that person going to be okay?! Are they? Wait, I have to be holding this synth pad in "Ashes to Ashes" soon, uh . . . yeah, they'll be okay! Right? I remember my bandmate next to me, the ever-fashionable Holly Palmer was dressed in a little blue outfit. She shuffled over to me during the concert saying how cold she was, but I smiled back at her, trying not to lose my place. The night air temperature was not on my radar. I was loving where I was. Glastonbury was a festival that I had dreamed of going to as an audience member, but there I was, singing so many fantastical songs with a legend who also happened to be a beautiful person. I remember, for that hour and a half, having the time of my life.

I remembered our voices. David's. Mine. Gail's. Holly's. The way our voices connected us onstage and the way they stretched out to the audience was like we were extending a helping hand or offering a warm embrace, from the gut, from our hearts. Our voices, things we use every day and take for granted, were amplified, soaring, and full of happiness and excitement. Then, that day at the table with the BLTs and my mom and Glasto on a laptop screen, it was as though I could see the last pieces of a puzzle coming into complete view. I saw myself bopping around onstage, a 25-year-old woman, vibrant, fearless, and ready to take on the world. I compared her to the person I now saw myself as — a mom worn down by the demands of life, a grief-stricken 40-year-old, a tired-out touring indie rocker, somebody's ex-wife picking up the pieces (and not well), a person who was ungratefully ho-humming about watching herself in a concert with David Bowie about to be released to the world!

I had to ask myself, shaking my head with tears in my eyes, What *on earth* happened? Where did I *go*? I felt a twinge of pain. This was no melancholic bid for the glory days of the past to return or a sorrowful pang of regret that I no longer had that baby face or the envy of my music industry peers. It all of a sudden dawned on me that I had misplaced myself. I had completely forgotten who I really was. Did I even know who I was?

One thing was for sure. I wanted to know that Emm who was onstage at Glasto. I wanted to recover the Emm who radiated that sense of possibility and that enraptured energy. She was still in me, I was sure of it. Maybe I had seen, heard, and felt myself in times when my voice emptied into a mic at home, when I lay my voice down like a calm lake like I did on my ambient album, like I did when I belted out the dregs of my pain on my song "Comets Call." Maybe, when I stood on the stage in London at the Grand Theatre, my true self popped out for a moment as I sung through the sass and poetry of "Coyote." As I admitted this to myself, and as I allowed myself to recognize where my true self had shown up over the years, even for a quick moment, I could see it clearly. My true self was in my singing. The most energetic, real version of me was present when surrounded by the joy of my voice.

ROCK 'N' ROLL SALVATION

One of those times when I felt completely myself was in 2015, when my rock band Trapper played arenas with Def Leppard. Trapper, a super-group of sorts, which I began with Canadian guitarist Sean Kelly, saw me as a front-person, dressed in rock attire and belting out hits while strutting around onstage and occasionally putting a foot up on the stage monitor to sing a blisteringly high note or two. If there was ever a time I was completely in my element, and completely myself, it was in this band. Surrounded by hearts of gold, brothers in rock 'n' roll, my voice stretched out across arenas, and I channeled all the glory of the 1980s as well as my female power. This was my dream.

I realized that whether it was singing with David, fronting Trapper, or singing my own songs at a grand piano in a theatre, my voice had carried me from childhood into a life of great experiences. I started to see salvation and beauty in voices everywhere. Freddie Mercury. Nina Simone. Aretha Franklin. In the speeches of great influencers of our time. In the voices of people everywhere fighting for change and equality. In the narrations of authors who knew about healing and female strength. As I stepped into realizing all the human voice could show me, about life and love, and myself, I began to teach people to sing, which was a next-level, abundant part of life that I hadn't planned for. Sharing what I knew about strengthening the voice and the voice's ability to give strength became incredibly fulfilling. The dots connected. My purpose became clear. The joy — palpable.

So, you may ask, how does returning to your true self have anything to do with being a great singer? You might even be able to list a thousand people who were lost and screwed up who had legendary voices. They sold lots of records and they influenced the world. They didn't take vocal lessons or sit around meditating; in fact some of them did cocaine off their nightstand before getting up in the morning. But that's the thing — being your true self doesn't mean doing all the things that I lay out in this book. **Being your true self is living by your own code.** It just so happens that living by my own code involved getting healthy enough to see my worth clearly. The perfection you seek is in what you may currently perceive as imperfection, and the easiest, quickest way to become a joyful singer and artist is to accept that you are different from the greatest opera singer in the world, that you sing differently than whoever is at the top of the charts, and that that's just amazing in itself. Your voice is a unique blueprint, and only you can figure out what needs to happen in your life to strengthen it and to set conditions for success. But the voice will always offer clues to the heart. And I do believe the action items in this book can bring positive, universal change because they're meant to unite you with the clues in your heart.

I believe that the events of those tumultuous few years, the loss of everything I thought was true, the deaths of two beautiful souls who lived their lives from a place of love and giving, and the flashback of Glastonbury, the chance to see myself sing at 25 — changed my perspective. Where I once took my voice and my gifts for granted, I suddenly accepted them and decided they were awesome. If my only dream as a child was to sing my own songs, to sing onstage and to go from being a terrible singer to a great one, I had done it! Had I spent the bulk of my life realizing it? Had I celebrated it? Had I taken my gift as far as I could? Had I allowed my voice to show me what I was capable of in my everyday life? No. But the minute I could see it, articulate it, and feel all the power and healing that my voice had to offer — I became energized.

ACTION ITEMS

1. **Make a list of the times you've felt most alive in your life.** Reflect on these — they are clues to what you need to be doing more of to return to your true self.

2. Recall a time when you felt total bliss, when the world fell away around you. We often refer to this as a state of flow. When we are *in flow* we are close to returning to that true self. **Name the activities that bring flow and build in time in your day, week, or month for them.**

3. **Refrain from comparing yourself to others.** "Compare despair," was something Coco, who worked with Bowie, once said to me. Make living consciously and with awareness your goal as opposed to constantly trying for a state of happiness. "I am enough" is a powerful phrase, which, when meditated upon, can bring liberation, ease, and contentment.

CHAPTER 21

HEALTHY, HEALTHY, HEALTHY

"To keep the body in good health is a duty . . . otherwise we shall not be able to keep our mind strong and clear."
— BUDDHA

Vocal health has an infinite number of layers. As I moved through life, I found even more things that helped me maintain good singing skill. Surprisingly, many of the things that I discovered extended beyond sleep, hydration, humidification, and so on. Taking health to the max involved choosing to live a certain way and with consistency.

ENERGY

We have a finite amount of energy. So many of us experience *energy leaks*. Energy leaks are places where you are spending time and effort on things that no longer serve your greater good. These can be choices we make related to habits, people we hang out with, and our own baggage. Maybe someone in your life who you have to see a lot continues to empty his negative rants out on you. Maybe you allow "friends" on social media to suck you into their world, and you absorb their views on politics and religion. The good news is, patching up the leaks can be one great way to really have success with your singing practice and your life in general. Fixing the leaks means you can spend energy on learning and living well instead of bitching about all the things that are interrupting your day and your flow. And guess who is in control of patching up those leaks or just walking away from them altogether? You guessed it: You.

Common places where energy leaks occur are:

1. when our own insecurities get regularly activated by interacting with certain people also known as "triggers,"
2. when we continually make choices that can't be sustained or lead to bad mental or physical health, and
3. when we surround ourselves with ingratitude, including negative people or people who have a critical, complaining take on life.

INSECURITIES

Insecurities run rampant for singers. Many people don't even bother singing at all just because of negative feedback received by peers or family in the early days of life. Because our brains were still in development, we were particularly susceptible to the criticism experienced in childhood and adolescence, and we have, in many cases, decided the harsh words we received are true. How incredibly unfair that adults knowingly or unknowingly influence children into believing they won't be good at something that they haven't even had a chance to explore! A good way to reverse some of the harmful feedback we've received regarding our voice, our bodies, our abilities, our dreams, and our musical goals is to stop giving the negative vibes power. There are a few ways to strip power from negativity:

1. **Distance yourself from the source of the negative feedback.** If this is someone like a family member or parent that you wouldn't cut out of your life, reframe the information they gave you. There are ways to reframe negative experiences and I encourage you to read up on them. Cognitive Behavioural Therapy, Cognitive Reframing, or methods for reframing trauma are all good ways to reverse powerful messages that have shaped us in life. You can also simply rewrite the story. Write a better ending to something negative that happened in your past. See how it brought you to a better place. Once you rewrite it, read it over and over and believe your new take.

2. **Take action.** This you've already done by picking up this book, reading the whole thing, and hopefully looking into getting a vocal coach and doing your exercises and action items. **Action creates motivation** so instead of wallowing in the bad vibes of the past, move your body, make noise, sing a note, and you'll find that small actions like

these will lead to more actions which will lead to a sense of feeling motivated.

3. **Block negative self-talk.** The cold hard truth: we are often the source of our energy leaks. We tell ourselves all kinds of things that are put-downs, imply we are inadequate, and reinforce our weaker selves. Some of us have done this for years. Practise stopping yourself before you say or think an unkind word about yourself. Catch yourself. Would you talk to your best friend the way you talk to yourself? The more you practise stopping yourself from negative self-talk, the more it will become painfully evident how often this happens in your life. Mindfulness and practise lead to change.

UNSUSTAINABLE CHOICES

We all make choices in our lives that we can't sustain. If we keep eating McDonald's hamburgers and fries, we'll feel pretty disgusting with every passing day. If we drive distracted, eventually, we'll injure or kill someone. If we drink a bottle of Scotch every night, we will eventually compromise our liver and run out of money — I don't know what's worse.

Let me share the example of smoking after my breakup. Although I gave myself the licence to feel the pain of heartbreak as long as I felt I needed to, I knew that after a while I would not be able to sustain the lifestyle of being a smoker. Not only would I smell bad, have dirty teeth, and increase my chance for heart disease or heart attack, but with every time I lit up, I'd be perpetuating that addiction. I'd be running out of money by buying smokes every week. I'd be compromising the instrument that my job as a performer was built around. I also knew that I'd set a bad example for my children and it wasn't the sort of habit I wanted as I worked to guide people toward nurturing their voices. To top it all off, my dad had produced a book when I was young called "The Only Way to Stop Smoking" and he had actually helped a few people to stop smoking. The dedication of this booklet bore the heartfelt line "to my children . . . may they never smoke." So, needless to say, every time I picked up a cigarette, I was met with a poop-storm of feelings of guilt, low self-worth, and disappointment in myself. Smoking was what I would call an unsustainable choice.

Quitting was dang hard. It involved a lot of stops and starts, a lot of talking myself out of doing it, downloading the app, and making a pact never to buy smokes again. **At the heart of it all is the need to get crystal clear on our values.** As I became more dedicated in my work as a coach, I realized that quitting smoking really was a non-negotiable thing for me. How could I lead others to greatness if I wasn't walking that walk?

I weaned myself off slowly. I also aligned the habit of smoking with more negative habits of other smokers I knew, such as an ex-boyfriend who couldn't see how awesome I was, so as I let go of that relationship, I quite easily let go of smoking. I haven't touched a cigarette in years. Do I get tempted? Not anymore. For a time I did, but when I did get tempted to pick it back up, it was back to that review of circumstances and sustainable choices. The questions, "What's really making me want this right now?" and "What will happen if I keep doing this?" became incredibly helpful when sorting through what to do and what not to do in life. Remember these two questions, they will be such a huge help the next time you're faced with a big decision. And when I'm talking about smoking, much of what I say can apply to any addiction, including phone use, shopping, gambling, the list goes on.

CULLING THE HERD

As creative people, we surround ourselves with all types of folks. Sometimes we open the door to people with different values than ours, and, more than often, it's not that the values are different, it's that others with whom we clash are unclear on their values. Sometimes they are unclear on being unclear on their values! As I covered earlier in the book, **when you're unclear on your values, your sense of integrity is compromised**. You lack that important mental document that tells you what you stand for and what you don't. Decision-making therefore becomes difficult, and boundaries are hard to set. When people can't make clear decisions or set clear boundaries, they can't have clear, respectful relationships. So one very big favour you can do yourself, and it's hard to do because sometimes it means a cull of friends, family, social media pals, and so on, is cutting people out who add nothing to your life, who suck the joy out, and who can't be trusted. Just make a clean cut. Life is short. You know instinctively who falls into the category of "joy-sucker" in your life. You know who the people are who talk about you behind your back. You know who the people are who operate from fear instead of love. You know who the people are who have opinions of you that are completely off-base. If you can't make a clean cut, set a boundary. Agree to be friendly, but don't agree to go on a two-week Mediterranean cruise with a joy-sucker and expect to feel good after.

When you surround yourself with people who are energized, who have great ideas, who are successful, prosperous, full of love and light, you too will find it easier to function in this way. Doesn't reading that list of descriptive words just make you feel good already? I'll list them again: people who are energized, who have great ideas, and who are successful, prosperous, and full of love and light. We need an environment of support as singers. We need this kind of energy as creative people. Because the singer's life can be so incredibly up and down, it's easy to fall prey to the hamster wheel of negativity. It's dang comfortable to stay in a place of pain and bitching about those ups and downs.

In my own life, I found a great way to focus on positive people and things was to simply turn the spotlight onto others. In those I am most energized by, I see joy, inquisitiveness, a desire to learn, and it makes me appreciate my own gifts so much more.

ACCOUNTABILITY

One of the biggest pitfalls in sticking to healthy choices is that we don't have someone in our corner to keep us on track. This is where creating a dream team of sorts can be very handy.

One of the reasons we show up at work is because we are being depended on to be present. The company or organization can't function if we roll in two hours late because we had to stop for a jumbo latte and vanilla scone. One of the reasons we have friends is because they depend on us, we won't let them down when they ask us to go for lunch. Trouble is, we struggle to bring this same accountability and respect to our own lives.

So? Create an accountability dream team: People to keep you on track with your healthy choices. This could be people you hire or it could be friends you ask for help. If clutter is an issue in your life, take a picture of a place that needs attention and send it to a friend and say, "Ask me to take this picture again in a month and send it to you." Or, hire a strategist or coach who can help you in your day-to-day life. This could be someone who works with you on nutrition, fitness, life stuff, or addiction. In AA, an alcoholic has a sponsor. In business, CFOs have assistants. At photo shoots, the videographer has a team. On the hockey rink, the coach switches out players to preserve the energy and effectiveness of the team. We are on the planet together, so we might as well make good use of each other and work together like we were meant to do.

CELEBRATE GOOD TIMES

Finally, when you have success, celebrate it!

As I started to focus more on sustainable choices, I noticed that alcohol was starting to interfere with everything important. Drinking made it difficult to be a great singer. Recovering from drinking the next day made singing very difficult due to fatigue and dehydration. Drinking made it difficult to be a good and patient mom. I noticed that alcohol was wrecking my sleep and exacerbating the mood swings of PMS. I also made the difficult decision to admit to myself that I had made a host of bad choices in my life due to drinking — everything from straying from my values to sometimes performing a show and not knowing what key I was in. As Malcolm Gladwell writes in *Talking to Strangers*, alcohol can have the tendency to make situations in life myopic. While buzzed, I had trouble zooming out and seeing the bigger picture, which for me is important.

I wondered why I had tolerated this behaviour from myself for so long. When I searched my soul, it became clear to me. I believed that if I didn't have alcohol coursing through my veins, I wouldn't be funny, I wouldn't be bad-ass, I wouldn't be sexy, rock 'n' roll, or dynamic as a performer. I really believed this for a long time. I wasn't a girl from Brooklyn raised by beat poets and change-makers, so I figured I need to find my coolness in a bottle of Talisker. Deep down, I knew it was all a crock of crap. I finally wondered if I could do what I perceived of as "interesting" with alcohol, could I find a way to do the same stuff without it? I asked myself on that topic of drinking irresponsibly, "What happens if I keep doing this?"

In February 2020, I made the decision to try to go without alcohol, one day at a time. It was simply time to start living and living cleanly. The first few weeks were difficult, but I reached out for help. I relied on apps, I met others who had given up drinking, I read other people's stories of sobriety, I went to an online meeting or two, and I talked it through with my therapist. But most importantly, I celebrated my milestones. One hundred days, three months, six months, one whole year! I also celebrated the strength in my voice and body. I fell in love with how quickly my voice warmed up and became powerful in its new state. There was no gunk, phlegm, or fatigue in my speaking and singing voice anymore. My liver was free to detoxify my skin. It took a while to see it, but my voice became stronger at 45 than it had been at 25 or 35. I celebrated the hell out of this. My biggest celebration occurred when my ten-year-old son said to me out of the blue one day in our kitchen, "Mom, I notice that you haven't yelled at us in a long time." Tears in my eyes, that was my trophy.

Today, as I write this, my choice to be healthy in my body and my voice has visible results. I don't strive for perfection, I strive for doing the best I can and making good choices. My children are thriving, beautiful humans and we are closer than ever before. Do I still feel overwhelmed as a parent? Sure, but I know how to apologize. I know how to be me. I know how to treat myself well, so I can show them how important it is that a woman treats herself with respect. I feel connected to my kids and it's not because I order them around (although I do sometimes) but because they are my teachers. My family is in a form I had not planned for it to be, but in many ways it is greater, more rich, multi-dimensional, calmer, more aware. By honouring my own gift to sing and letting my voice take me into a realm of healing, I have been able to see my family as a spiritual unit, where everyone has something to learn and give. The pain of my divorce has healed with time. I realize that the past is the past and I won't drag my present through it. I took my own advice from the last chapter and rewrote my story. I wrote a thank you to what the universe handed me because I was able to move into a place of self-love. Is everything rainbows and roses? Yes! Even in the challenges there can be joy, humour, and awakening. Look at Viktor Frankl who found humour, light, and love in the darkest recesses of the Holocaust. This is not meant to belittle the tragedies of humanity, it is meant to shine a light on the fact that you are stronger than you believe. You are more lovable than you are willing to admit. Listening to your body, your voice, and your musical desires can literally change your world. Focusing on creativity and singing, and making the choice to move out of victim mode, can put you in a place of power, forgiveness, and possibility. With these doors open, there's been so much love, friendship, laughter, success, and joy able to come through. I know that you will find this too.

ACTION ITEMS

1. **Patch up energy leaks.** Your success as a singer depends on it. Use this to remember how to easily soar past the energy drains in your life: Distance, Take Action, Then Practise. Distance yourself from the negative person or action and then do something to advance your craft. If you're the source of the negativity, practise speaking and thinking kindly of yourself by *stopping* yourself before you say or think something crappy.

2. **Name one area in your life where you can be doing better in terms of health.** Ask yourself about this unhealthy habit or unfavourable thing, "What will happen if I keep doing this?" Then, name one small action you can take to step into a healthier mindset and healthy actions as it relates to this area.

3. **Create some accountability around this one thing that you want to improve upon.** Ask a friend to be on your accountability team. Make sure they'll hold you to some advancement in this area. Make sure you adore and admire this friend, or you won't stay accountable to them.

4. **Ditch the people with bad vibes** or simply create a boundary where you interact with them less. There's no need to do this in a mean or rude way, it's just a way to maintain your own self-respect and self-care. Don't expect them to understand.

5. **Name and celebrate one thing you've done in your life that has moved you into a healthy place.** You've likely already done a lot of these things, so if you have more than one, list them and then reward yourself for these accomplishments.

CHAPTER 22

LAST WORD

"When we are aligned and in balance with our heart, we can open to the mysteries of life and the healing power of love."
— LAUREN MONROE

I was raised to be nice. My mom, Linda, has always led a life of charity and generosity. "Always do the right thing," she said to me when I was a kid, advice that would have made me sigh, empty a box of Nerds down my throat, and walk away from with eyes rolling. To me, doing the right thing in my teenage years and twenties meant following my passion. Dressing up, writing songs, singing them, and basking in the spotlight. I dreamed I'd have a voice with which I could top the charts, collect Grammys, and show my high school comrades that I was more than just a music geek who could play the entire *Seventh Son of a Seventh Son* album on my electric bass. I did everything I could to find that record deal, to find success, and to keep my creative spirit energized and alive. And yes, I got the deal.

I found the success and I felt alive. But it was only when young Emee Fink came to me for that first singing lesson that anything began to make sense to me. As I started to teach and to share my knowledge, I started to appreciate my voice, fall in love with my own path, a path that had started while I cleaned chicken poop off eggs and sang my own songs quietly in my bedroom. I started to love seeing others thrive. As I celebrated them, I celebrated myself — in a new light.

Giving back opened up another door to me, the door of sharing, of authentically caring about others, of experiencing newly rediscovered beauty in the voices of others. Because I had worked so hard to bring my voice out of the shadows, I could see that it really was true: That anyone can sing.

Secret No. 25: Give back.

In late June 2020, as the world saw us self-quarantining and isolating to keep COVID-19 virus cases down, the BBC aired the highlights of various Glastonbury concerts from over the years. The landmark concert I did with David and the band would be aired to all of Britain in its entirety for free alongside classic performances by Lady Gaga, Beyoncé, The Cure, and The Killers. With nowhere to go, music-lovers everywhere could hunker down with their families, their partners, their pets to take in four days of amazing live music from their homes. Although those concerts were meant to be experienced in the crisp air of the countryside, in the company of others, I felt so delighted that our concert would finally be shown to so many people, especially at a time when live music and its fate hung in the balance.

I spent the early morning hours of June 28, 2020, reflecting on the concert. Glastonbury had been such a big part of David's life. Perhaps the festival performances — 1971 and 2000 — had been like bookends for him. And man, how it had been like bookends for me when Parlophone released the concert and my 40-something self watched my 20-something self with awe and reckoning. I remembered something David had said to us, the band, on the way into the festival grounds. It wasn't something I had thought of very much, but for some reason, it came to my mind. David said to us of the mammoth, overflowing Glastonbury crowd, "This isn't about us, it's about them." His words underscored this world that I now moved through with awareness, grace, and gratitude.

As that summer began, I felt him with me for a moment, his spirit floating around, still jazzed by indie music and fashion and art and laughter. I imagined him being back on Earth just for a spell. He'd acknowledge the lost state of the world — upheaval on the streets of America, chaos in the White House, disease crawling over our planet, bedlam on the internet — and he'd do it in his own way with brushstrokes of lightness and empathy, and maybe even through music — more strung-out horns and dizzying beats. I'm sure he'd wrap his voice around the mayhem if he could. He'd champion the notion that no one really knows what they're doing anyway. But he'd keep moving.

Of all the rules and lessons and things I've learned as a singer and a musician, the one thing that keeps coming back to me is the thing that makes everything possible in the first place: breath. Breath has been with us in our first moments and it'll be there till our last living second. Breath fuels the sounds, the music, the voices that change our world, and it rescues us when we are panicked, abandoned, and alone.

A LONG EXHALE

One night when I was a little girl, my dad sat next to my bed and told me about breathing. It was the first I had ever heard anyone talk about deep breathing. Likely, it had been something that had served him well to manage anxiety and nerves. I remember him telling me that deep breathing would help me through my whole life, and he showed me some simple breathing exercises. This little bit of wisdom was something I filed away and kept with me, only really examining its power and poignancy recently. Dad was right. A deep breath in, a long hold, and a long exhale brings calm, possibility, transformation, and lightness. Every time.

Breathing in, and breathing out. Taking, and giving back. *It's not about us, it's about them.* What is magical about the voice is the breath that lies beneath it — an invisible, omnipresent life-force that makes something from seemingly nothing. On breath we find the words of poets, the songs of survivors, the cries of injustice, or the wishes of a child. In the ultimate show of the body's gift for giving, the breath carries the voice perfectly, like lovers and best friends carry one another, through good, through bad, and through everything in between.

But the breath should be a deep one. The voice should be full. The heart should give its all. And as Mary Oliver asked the world, so can you ask yourself from time to time: "Listen, are you breathing just a little and calling it a life?"

THE 25 SECRETS
OF SINGING

1. Rediscover your breathing.
2. Singing is a sport.
3. Stay curious.
4. You'll be able to forget this stuff one day.
5. See it all happening.
6. You need a good vocal coach.
7. Set the conditions for success.
8. Warm up!
9. Relax, just do it.
10. Get out there!
11. Know your why.
12. Be open to anything.
13. You're a singer all day long.
14. Know your values and know what you need.
15. Your power is in you.
16. Focus the sound.
17. Let go.
18. Stretch yourself.
19. Failure is an opportunity.

20. Run an honest business.
21. Surround yourself with stars.
22. Ask for help.
23. Watch and listen to yourself.
24. Sing with a solid tone.
25. Give back.

ACKNOWLEDGEMENTS

The author would like to thank: Susan Charles, Michael Colford, Laura Curtis, the Dafoe family (especially Tracie and Lauren), john r. durand, Deni and Angie Gauthier, the Gryner family (Tony, Frank, Jim, and Linda), Chris and Helene Hadfield, Peter Janes, Sean and Erin Kelly, Steve Kenny, Darryl Lahteenmaa, Patrick Lowe, Sandra Merzib, Catherine Pan and Steve Gammon, Elizabeth Mitchell, Jeff Robb, Emily Schultz, and Mitch Seekins. To Dave Bidini, for listening to my idea for this book before anyone else and to Michael Holmes for everything.

RECOMMENDED READING

Bel Canto: A Theoretical and Practical Vocal Method by
    Mathilde Marchesi
Man's Search For Meaning by Viktor Frankl
You Can Heal Your Life by Louise L. Hay
The Abundance Code by Julie Ann Cairns
*The Conscious Parent: Transforming Ourselves, Empowering
    Our Children* by Dr. Shefali Tsabary
*The Four Tendencies: The Indispensable Personality Profiles
    That Reveal How to Make Your Life Better (and Other
    People's Lives Better, Too)* by Gretchen Rubin
The Richest Man in Babylon by George S. Clason
The Science of Getting Rich by Wallace D. Wattles
*The Soul of Money: Transforming Your Relationship with
    Money and Life* by Lynne Twist
*The Soulful Journey of Recovery: A Guide to Healing from a
    Traumatic Past for ACAs, Codependents or Those with
    Adverse Childhood Experiences* by Dr. Tian Dayton
Think and Grow Rich by Napoleon Hill
You Are a Badass at Making Money by Jen Sincero

ABOUT THE AUTHOR

Emm Gryner is one of the first Canadian recording artists to start her own independent record label. She is a singer, multi-instrumentalist, coach, and former CBC radio host. She has been nominated three times for a Juno Award and twice for Pop Album of The Year. Emm toured the world and appears on recordings with David Bowie, including "Bowie at The Beeb" and "Glastonbury 2000." In 2013, Emm collaborated with astronaut Chris Hadfield on his version of "Space Oddity," recorded partially aboard the International Space Station. The Hadfield-Gryner version has received over 200 million views worldwide and is celebrated as the first music video recorded in outer space. Emm is Mom to Ronan and Aoife, partner to Michael, and cat-mom to Izzy.

This book is also available as a Global Certified Accessible™ (GCA) ebook. ECW Press's ebooks are screen reader friendly and are built to meet the needs of those who are unable to read standard print due to blindness, low vision, dyslexia, or a physical disability.

Get the eBook free!*
*proof of purchase required

Purchase the print edition and receive the eBook free!
Just send an email to ebook@ecwpress.com and include:

• the book title
• the name of the store where you purchased it
• your receipt number
• your preference of file type: PDF or ePub

A real person will respond to your email with your eBook attached. And thanks for supporting an independently owned Canadian publisher with your purchase!